easy piano

TOP HITS OF 2013

ISBN 978-1-4803-5488-3

7777 W. BLUEMOUND RD. P.O. BOX 13819 MILWAUKEE, WI 53213

Visit Hal Leonard Online at
www.halleonard.com

BLURRED LINES

Words and Music by PHARRELL WILLIAMS
and ROBIN THICKE

and that's why I'm gon' take ya,   good   girl.   I know you want it,

I know you want it.   I know you want it. You're a   good   girl.

Can't let it get past me.   You're far from plas- tic.   Talk a-bout get-tin' blast- ed. Hate these

blurred lines.   I know you want it,   I know you want it,

I know you want it. You're a good girl. The way you grab me,

must wan-na get nas-ty. Go a-head, get at me. What do they make dreams for

when you got them jeans on? What do we need steam for? You the hot-test one in this place.

I feel so luck-y, hey, hey, hey. You wan-na hug me, hey, hey,

D.S. al Coda

hey. What rhymes with hug me? Hey, hey,   hey. _____

CODA

Ev'rybody get up.

Hey, hey, hey.   Hey, hey, hey.   Hey, hey,

hey.

CRUISE

Words and Music by CHASE RICE,
TYLER HUBBARD, BRIAN KELLEY,
JOEY MOI and JESSE RICE

Ba - by, you a song, you make me wan - na roll my win - dows down and

cruise.

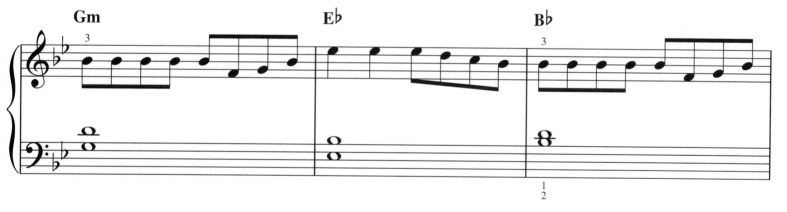

Yeah, when

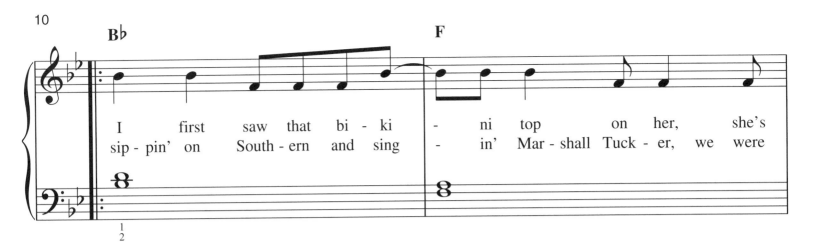

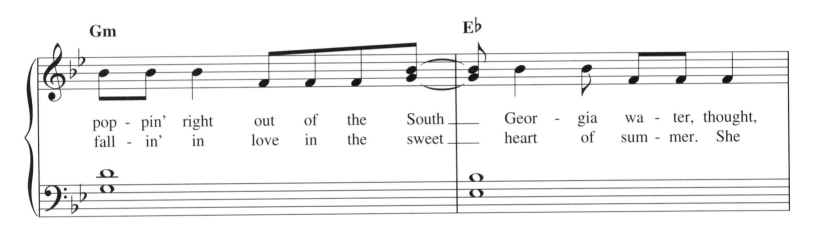

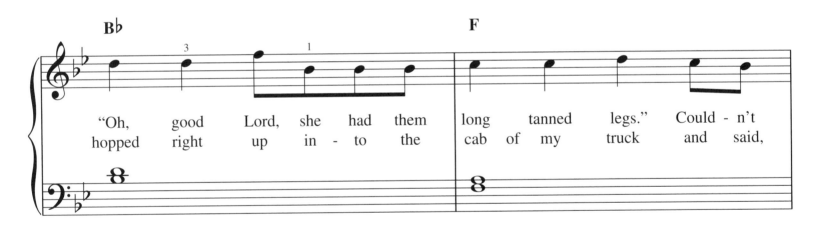

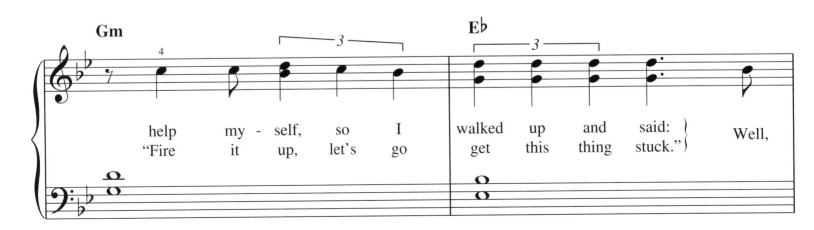

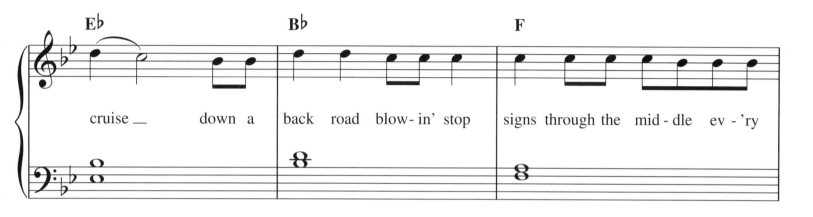

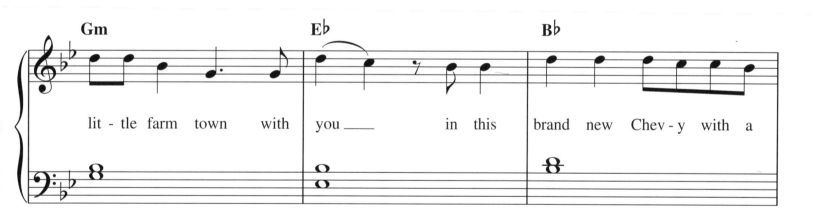

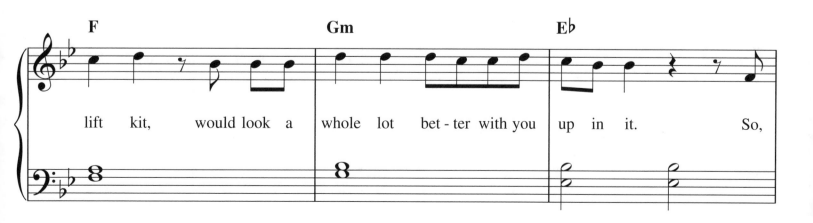

ba - by, you a song, you make me wan-na roll my win-dows down and

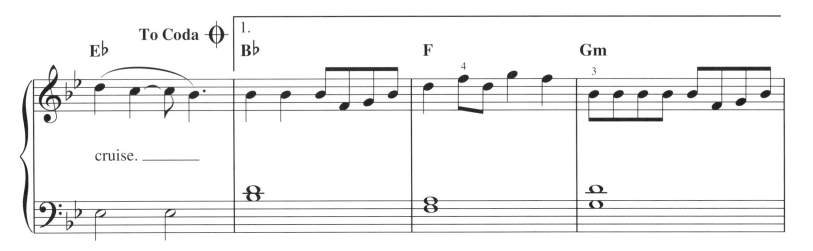

cruise. _____

Well, she was

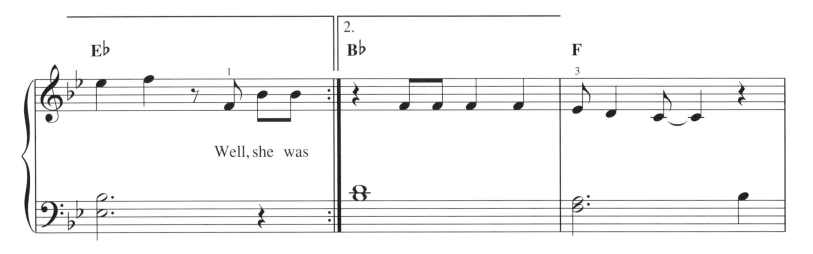

When that ___ sum - mer sun fell

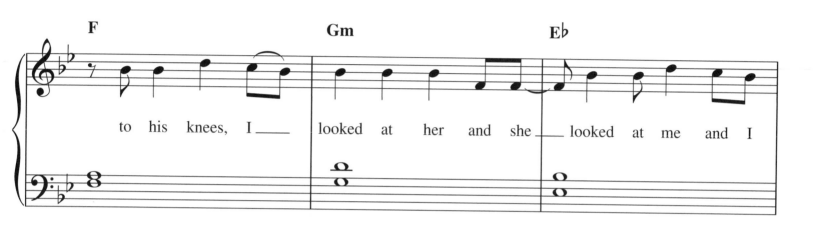

to his knees, I ___ looked at her and she ___ looked at me and I

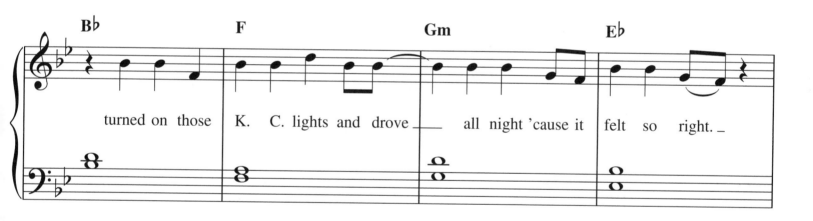

turned on those K. C. lights and drove ___ all night 'cause it felt so right. ___

Her and I, man, we felt ___ so right. ___ I put it in park and grabbed ___

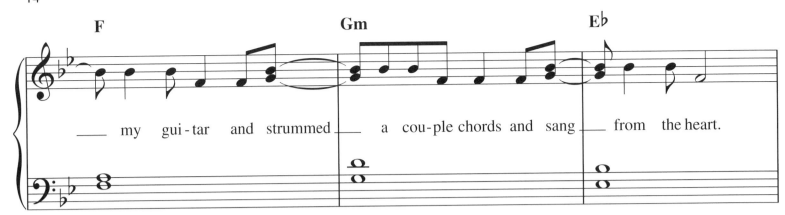

_____ my gui - tar and strummed _____ a cou - ple chords and sang _____ from the heart.

Girl, you sure _____ got the beat in my chest bump - in'. Hell, I can't get you

out - ta my head. Ba - by, you a song, you make me wan - na roll my

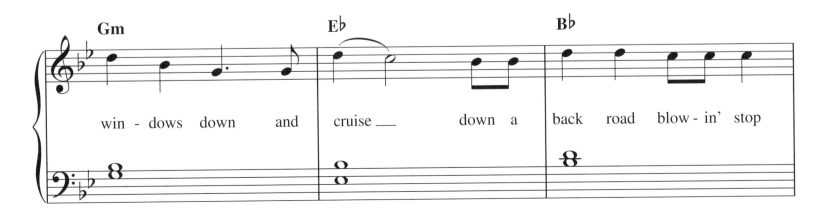

win - dows down and cruise _____ down a back road blow - in' stop

F   Gm   E♭   **D.S. al Coda**

signs through the mid - dle ev - 'ry   lit - tle farm town   with   you. ___   Well,

CODA   B♭   F   Gm

Get those

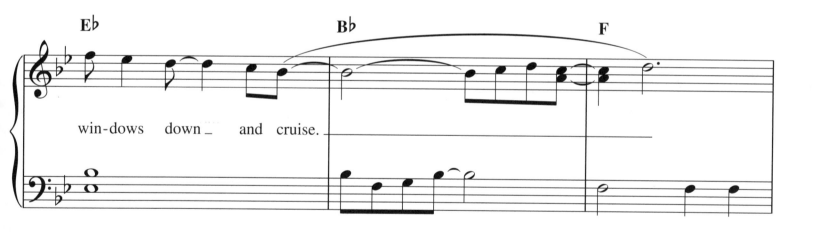

E♭   B♭   F

win-dows down __ and cruise. _____

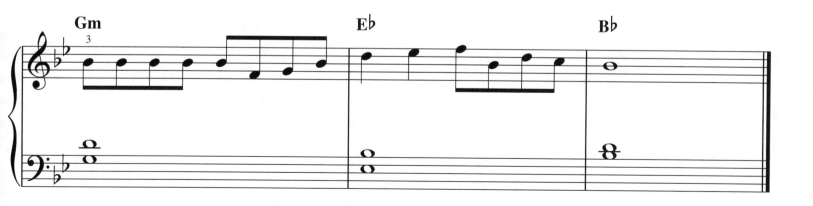

Gm   E♭   B♭

CALL ME MAYBE

Words and Music by CARLY RAE JEPSEN,
JOSHUA RAMSAY and TAVISH CROWE

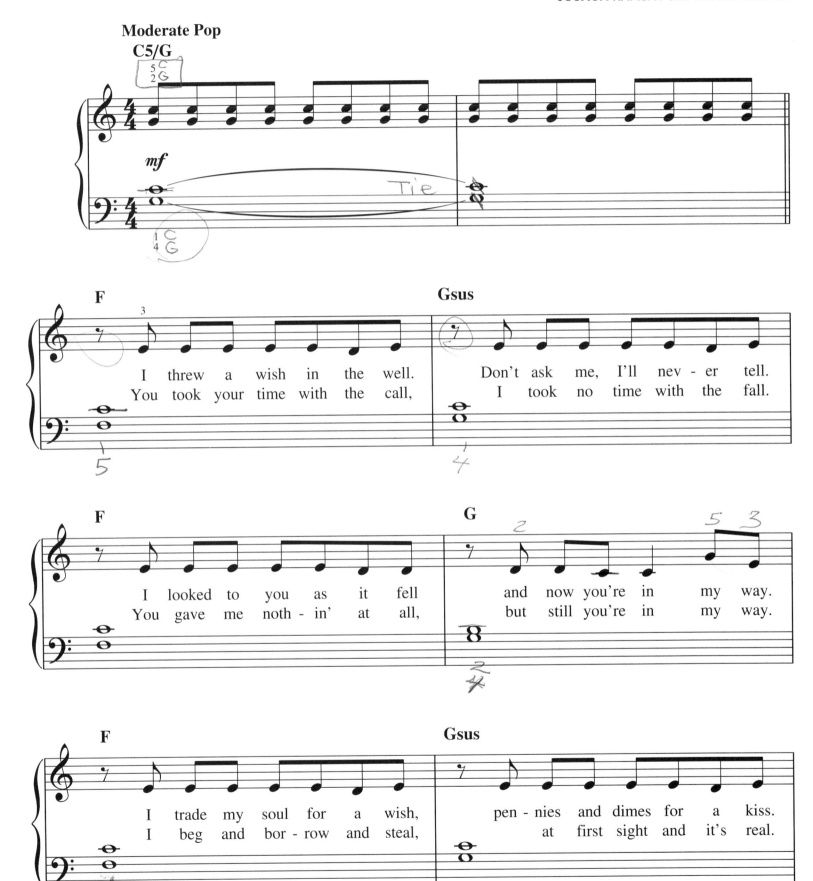

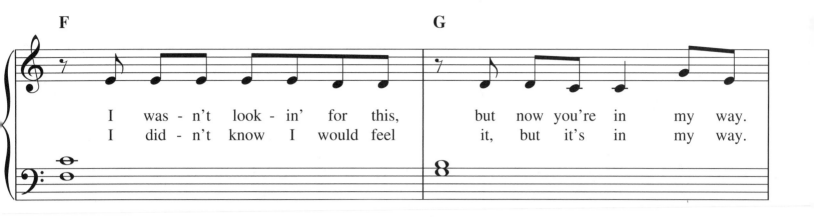

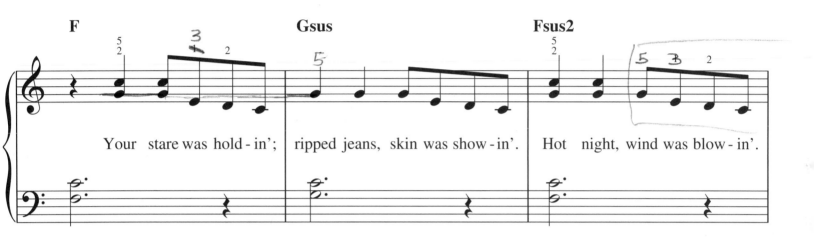

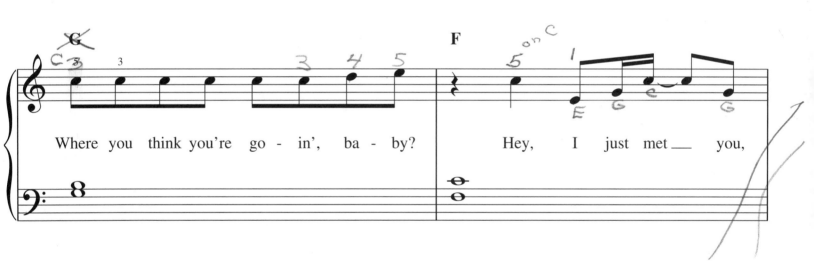

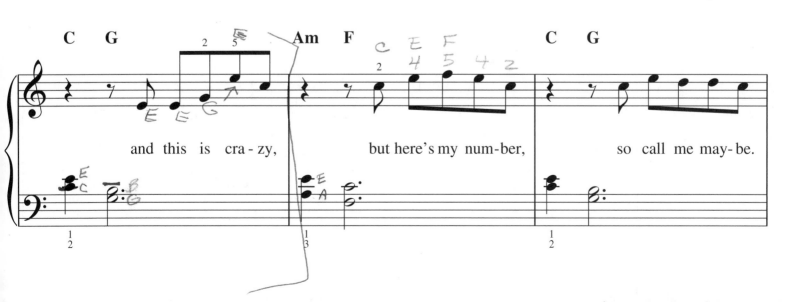

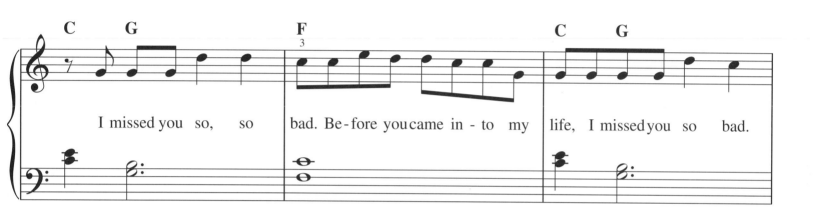

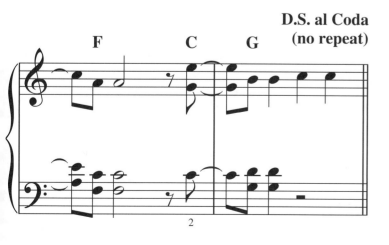

CATCH MY BREATH

Words and Music by KELLY CLARKSON,
JASON HALBERT and ERIC OLSON

Moderate Dance beat

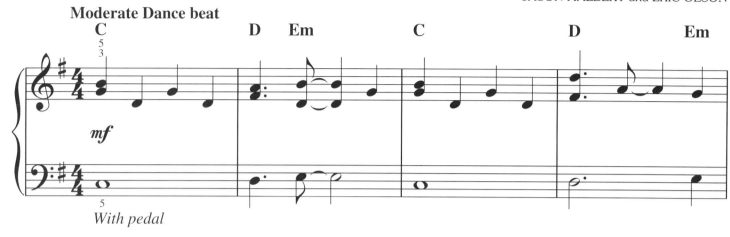

I don't want to be left _

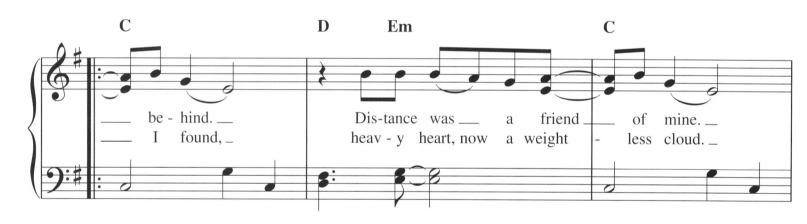

_ be - hind. _
_ I found, _

Dis - tance was _ a friend _ of mine. _
heav - y heart, now a weight - less cloud. _

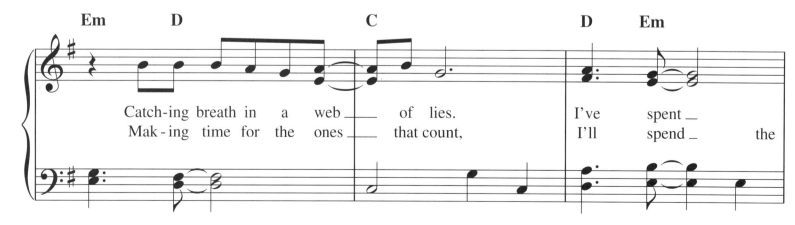

Catch - ing breath in a web _ of lies.
Mak - ing time for the ones _ that count,

I've spent _
I'll spend _ the

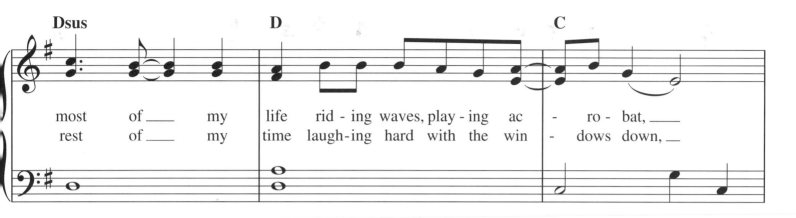

most of ___ my life rid - ing waves, play - ing ac - ro - bat, ____
rest of ___ my time laugh-ing hard with the win - dows down, __

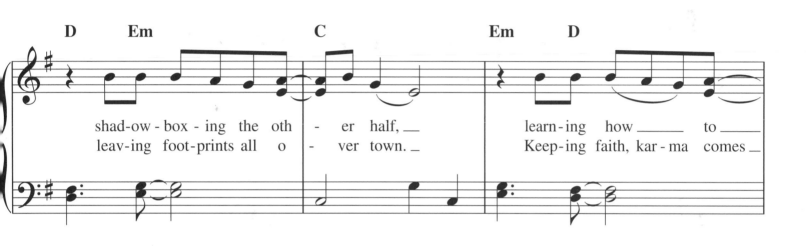

shad-ow - box - ing the oth - er half, __
leav-ing foot-prints all o - ver town. _

learn - ing how _____ to _____
Keep-ing faith, kar - ma comes _

___ re - act.
___ a - round.

I've spent _ most of ___ my
I'll spend _ the rest of ___ my

time...
life... Catch-ing my breath, let - ting it go, turn - ing my

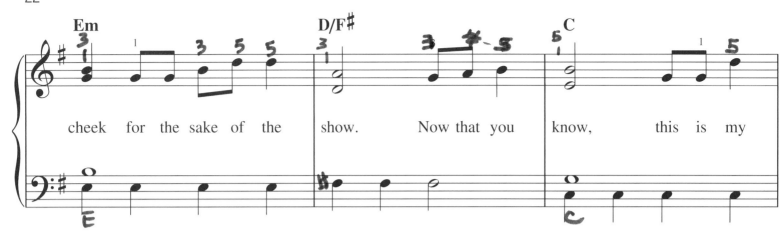

cheek for the sake of the show. Now that you know, this is my

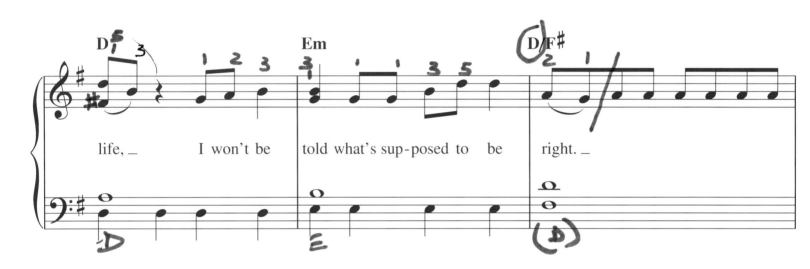

life, __ I won't be told what's sup-posed to be right. __

Catch my __ breath, __ no one can hold me back. __ I ain't got time for that. __

Catch my __ breath, __ won't let 'em get me down. __

It's all so sim-ple now. _ Ad-dict-ed to the love _ You

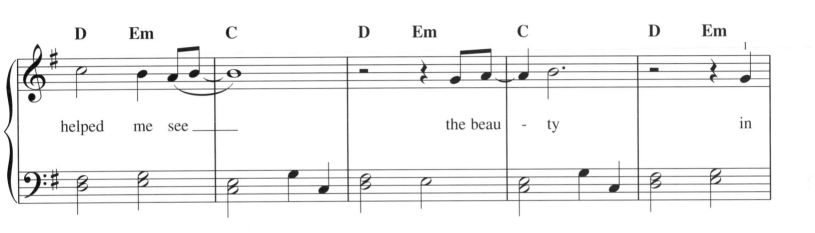

helped me see _ the beau - ty in

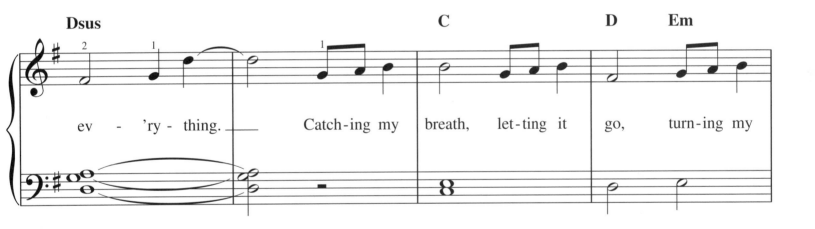

ev - 'ry - thing. _ Catch-ing my breath, let-ting it go, turn-ing my

cheek for the sake of the show. Now that you know, this is my

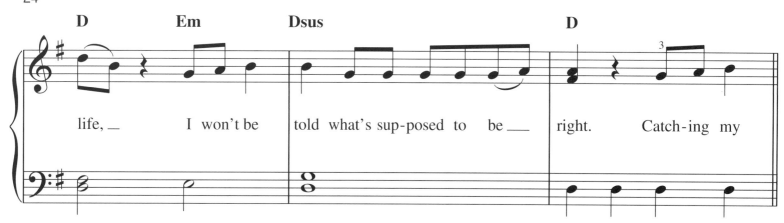

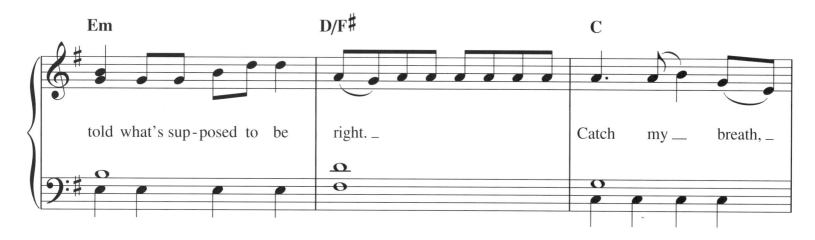

no one can hold me back. _ I ain't got time for that. _

Catch my _ breath, _ won't let 'em get me down. _ It's all so sim-ple now. _

Catch-ing my

rit.

HEART ATTACK

Words and Music by JASON EVIGAN,
MITCH ALLAN, SEAN DOUGLAS,
NIKKI WILLIAMS, AARON PHILLIPS
and DEMI LOVATO

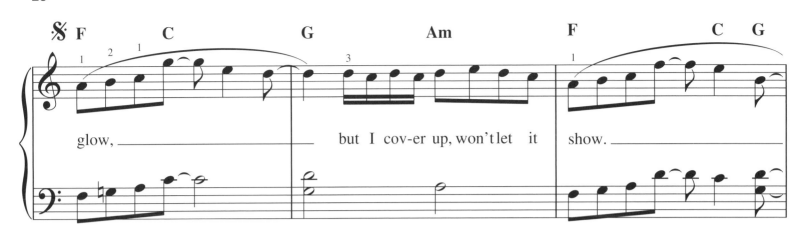

glow, _____ but I cov-er up, won't let it show. _____

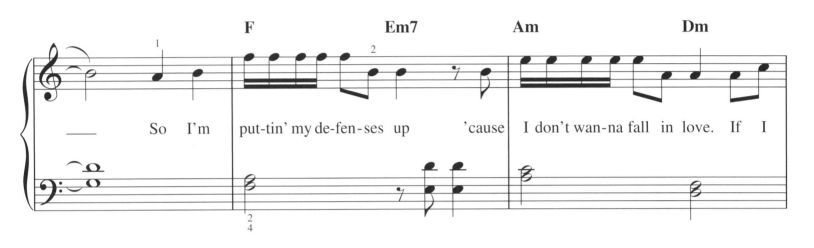

_____ So I'm put-tin' my de-fen-ses up 'cause I don't wan-na fall in love. If I

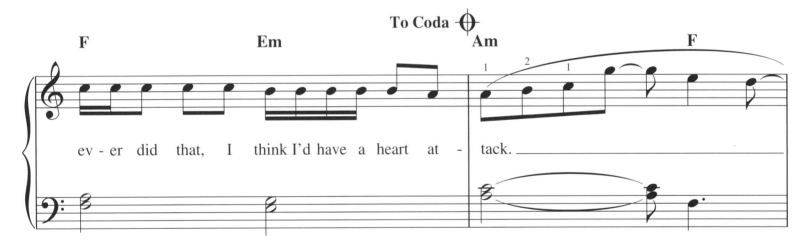

ev - er did that, I think I'd have a heart at - tack. _____

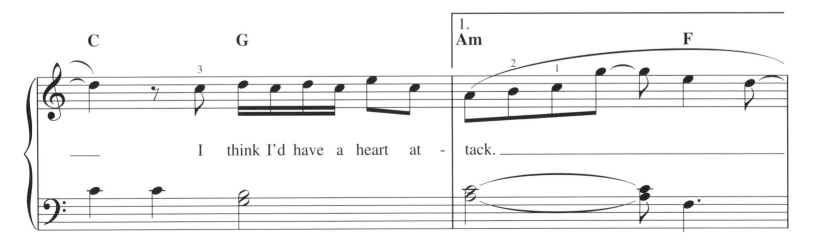

I think I'd have a heart at - tack. _____

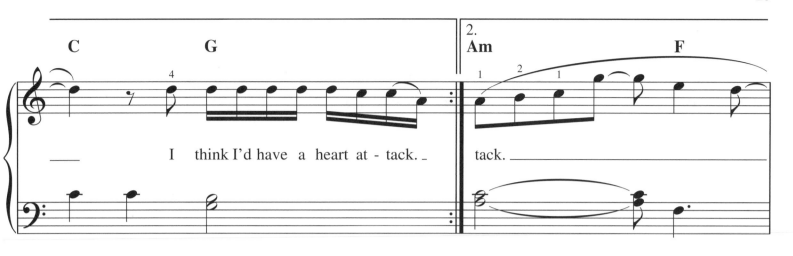

I think I'd have a heart at - tack. ___ tack. _____

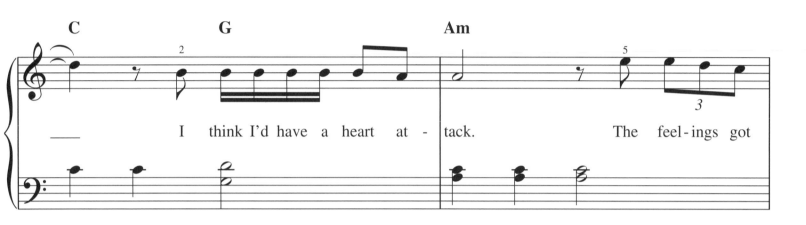

I think I'd have a heart at - tack. _____ The feel - ings got

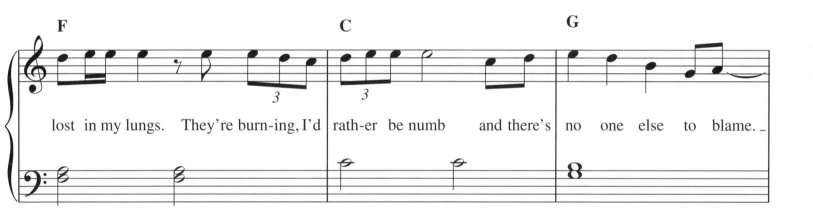

lost in my lungs. They're burn-ing, I'd rath-er be numb and there's no one else to blame. __

___ So scared I take off in a run. I'm fly - ing too

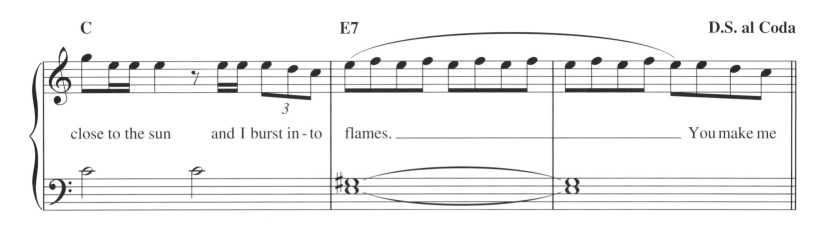

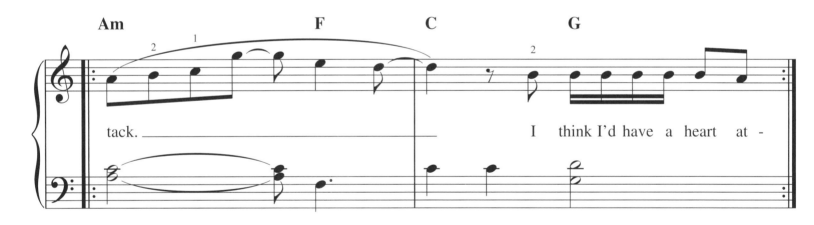

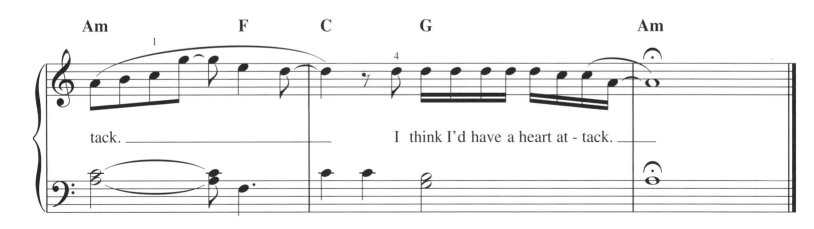

DAYLIGHT

Words and Music by ADAM LEVINE,
MAX MARTIN, SAM MARTIN
and MASON LEVY

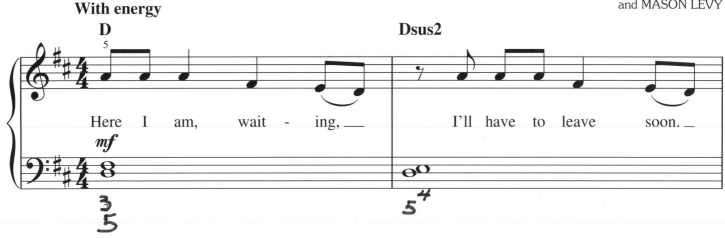

Here I am, wait-ing, __ I'll have to leave soon. __

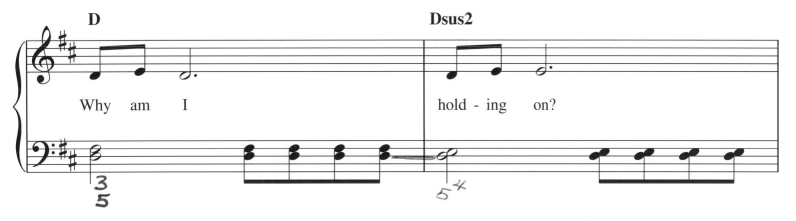

Why am I hold-ing on?

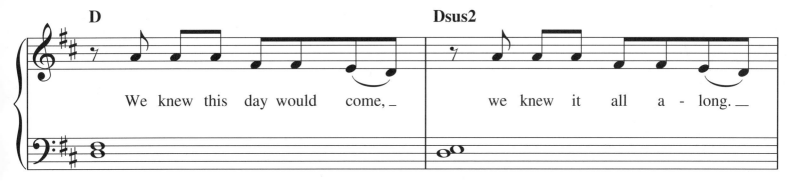

We knew this day would come, __ we knew it all a-long. __

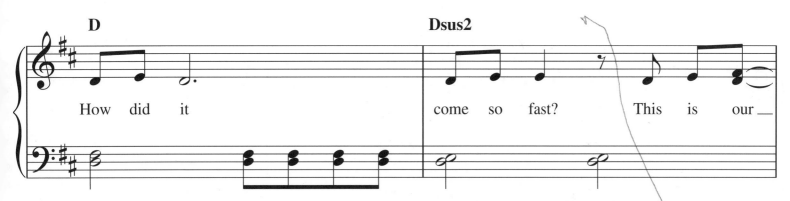

How did it come so fast? This is our __

last night, but it's late ___ and I'm try -

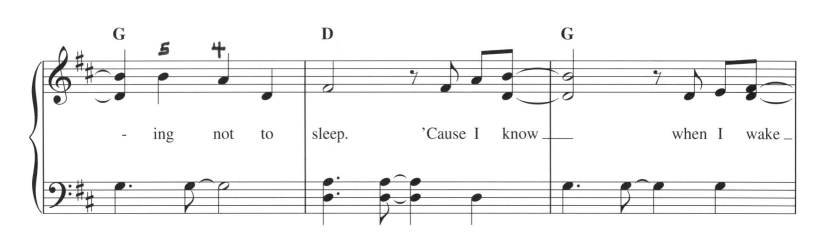

- ing not to sleep. 'Cause I know ___ when I wake _

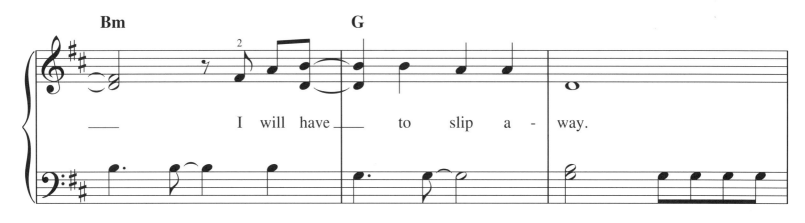

___ I will have ___ to slip a - way.

And when the day - light comes I'll have to go, but to - night _

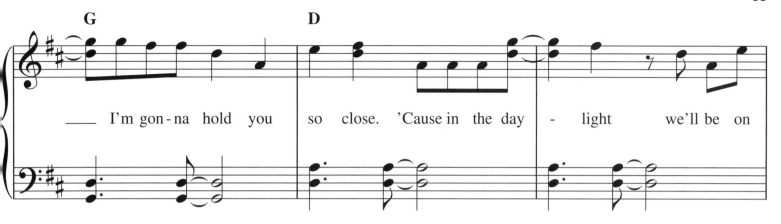

G   D

_____ I'm gon-na hold you so close. 'Cause in the day - light we'll be on

Bm   G   D

our own, but to - night ____ I need to hold you so close. Oh. ____

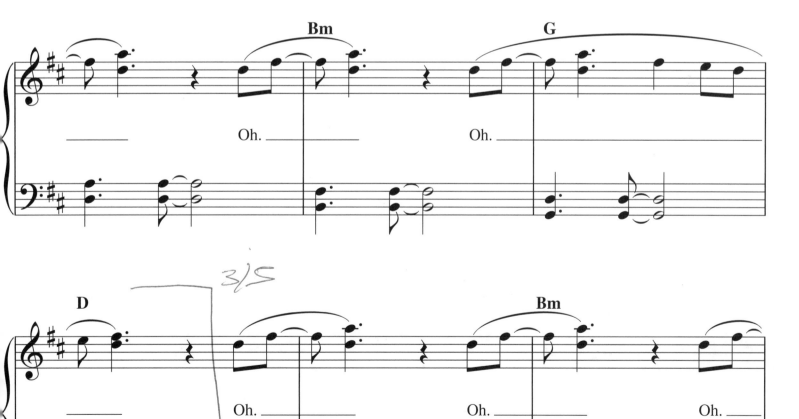

Bm   G

_____ Oh. ____ Oh. ____

D   Bm

_____ Oh. ____ Oh. ____ Oh. ____

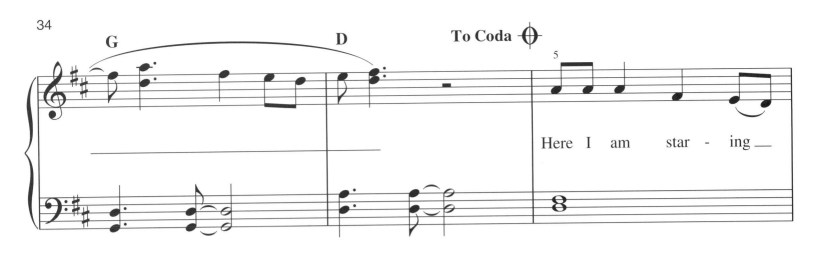

G   D   To Coda

Here I am star - ing ___

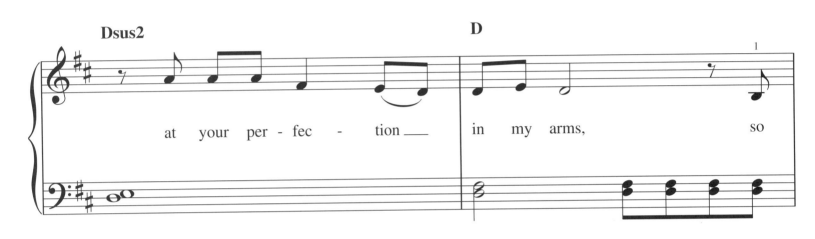

Dsus2   D

at your per - fec - tion ___ in my arms, ___ so

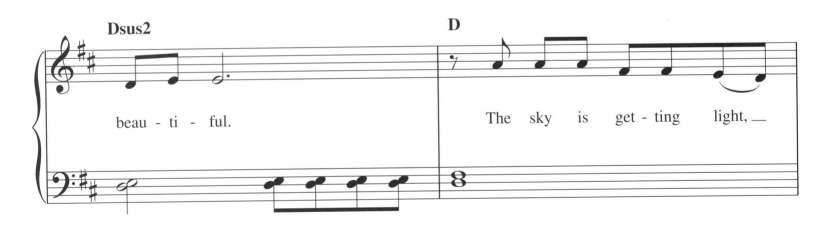

Dsus2   D

beau - ti - ful.   The sky is get - ting light, ___

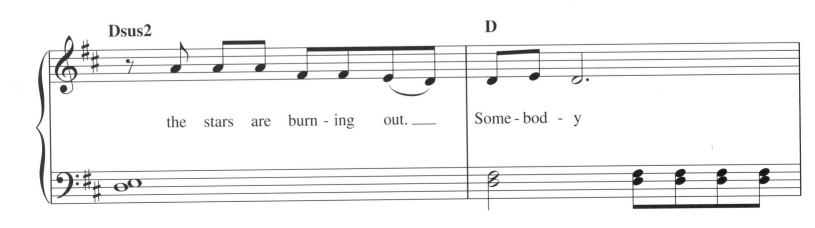

Dsus2   D

the stars are burn - ing out. ___ Some - bod - y

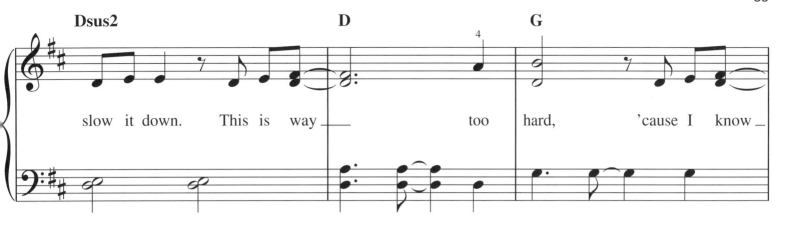

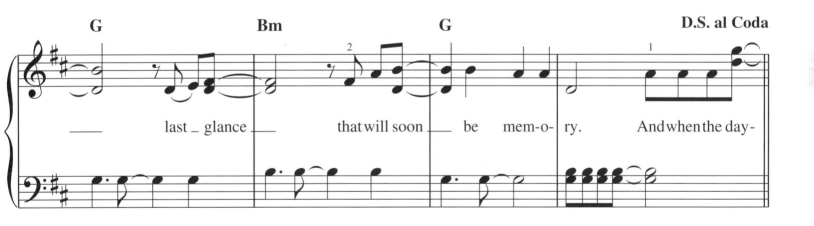

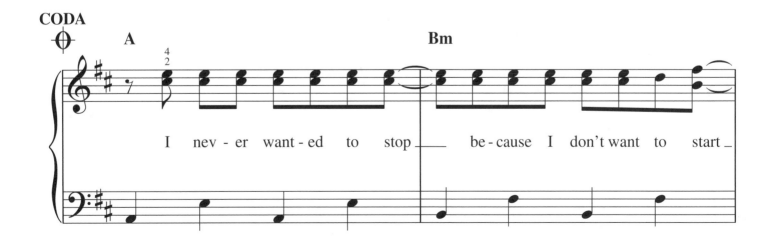

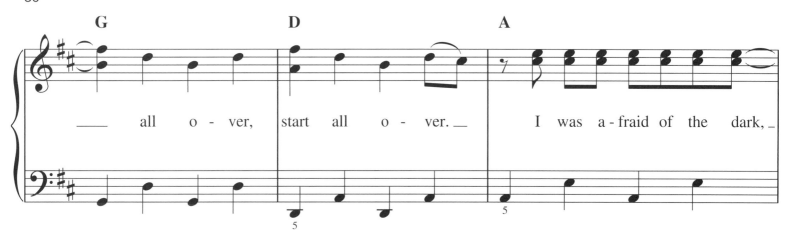

GET LUCKY

Words and Music by THOMAS BANGALTER,
GUY MANUEL HOMEM CHRISTO, PHARRELL WILLIAMS
and NILE RODGERS

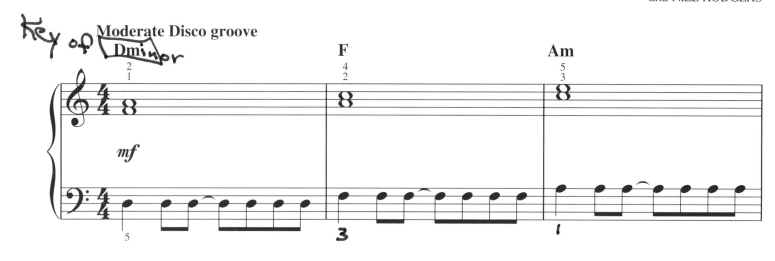

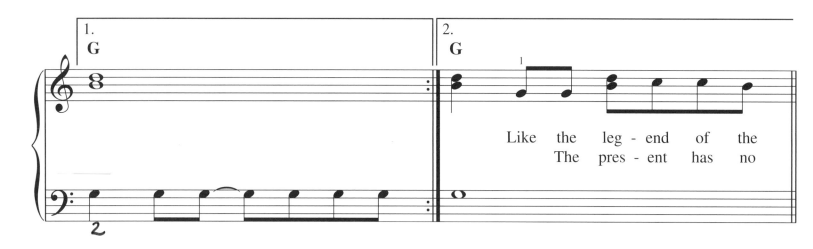

Like the leg-end of the
The pres-ent has no

Phoe-nix, _____
liv-ing, _____

all ends with be-on
your gift keeps on

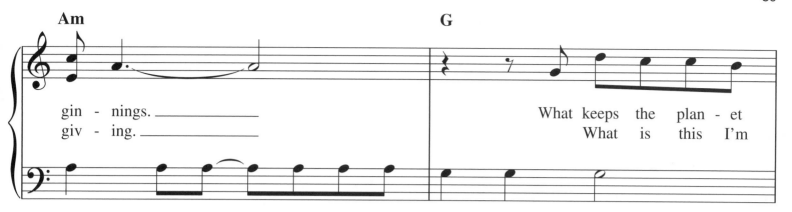

So let's _____ raise the bar ___

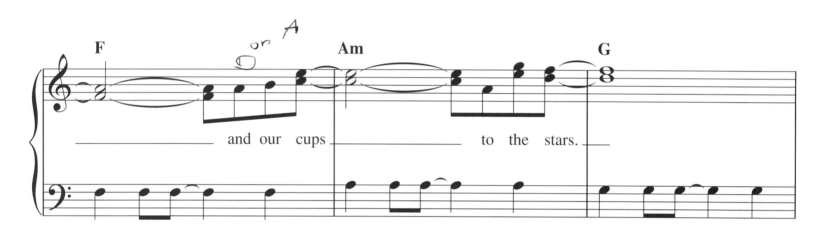

_____ and our cups _____ to the stars. ___

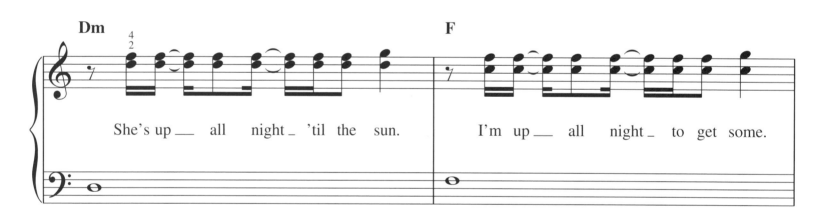

She's up ___ all night ___ 'til the sun.   I'm up ___ all night ___ to get some.

She's up ___ all night ___ for good fun.   I'm up ___ all night ___ to get luck - y.

42

We're up ___ all night ___ to get luck - y.   We're up ___ all night ___ to get luck - y.

GONE, GONE, GONE

Words and Music by GREGG WATTENBERG,
DEREK FUHRMANN and TODD CLARK

46

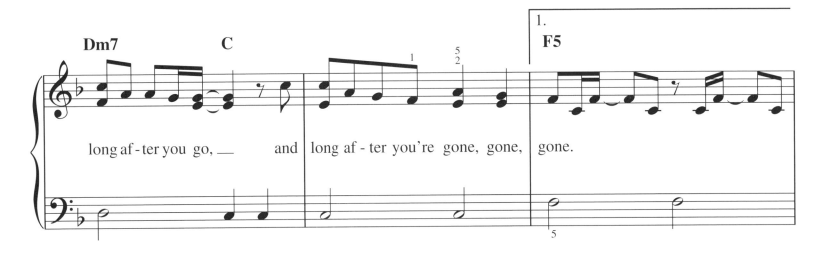

B♭sus2   **Dm7**

_____ you're my crutch when my legs stop mov - ing. You're my head start, _

F   **B♭sus2**

_____ you're my rug - ged heart, _____ you're the pulse that I've al - ways need - ed.

F   **Dm7**   **Csus**   **B♭sus2**   **F**

Like a drum, ba - by, don't stop beat - in'. Like a drum, ba - by,

Dm7   **Csus**   **B♭sus2**   **F**   **Dm7**   **Csus**

don't stop beat - in'. Like a drum, ba - by, don't stop beat - in'.

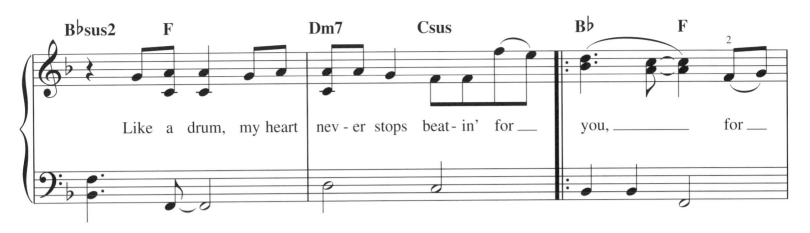

Like a drum, my heart nev - er stops beat - in' for __ you, _____ for __

you. ____ Ba - by, I'm __ not mov - ing on, I'll love you long __ af - ter you're gone. For __

you, _____ for __ you. ____ You will nev - er sleep a - lone; _ I'll love you

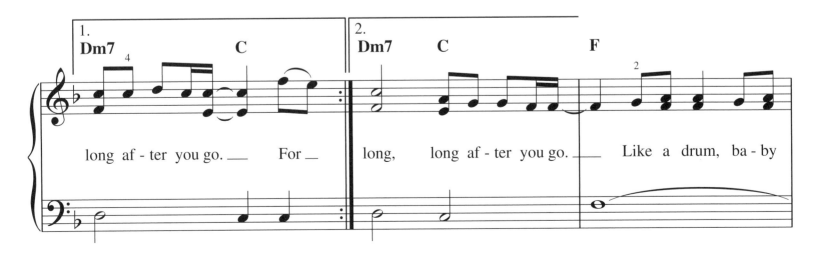

long af - ter you go. ___ For __ long, long af - ter you go. __ Like a drum, ba - by

don't stop beat - in'. Like a drum, ba - by, don't stop beat - in'.

Like a drum, ba - by, don't stop beat - in'. Like a drum, my heart

nev - er stops beat - in' for you. And long af - ter you're gone, gone,

gone. I'll love you long af - ter you're gone, gone, gone.
rit.

I WILL WAIT

Words and Music by
MUMFORD & SONS

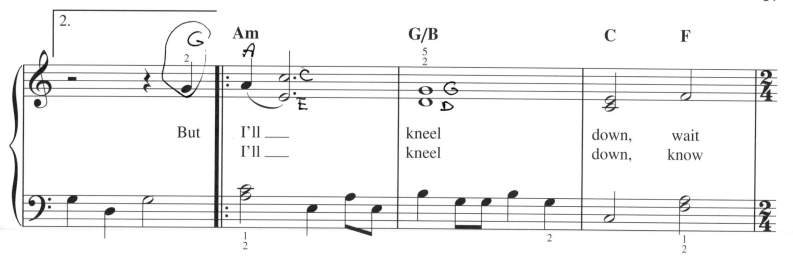

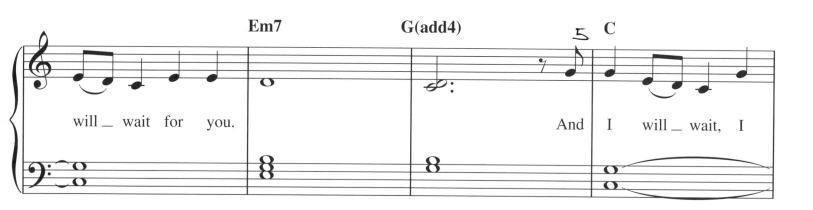

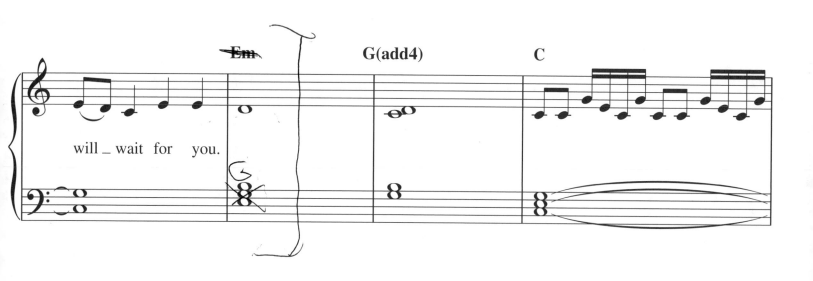

So break my

C   F

step   and re -   lent. _____
seen   and him with   less. _____

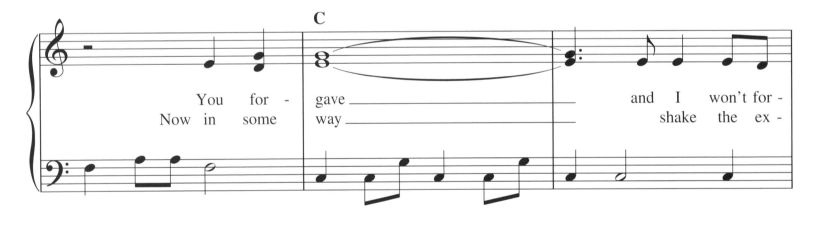

C

You for - gave _____   and I won't for -
Now in some way _____   shake the ex -

G   1.   2.

get.   Know what we've
cess.   'Cause

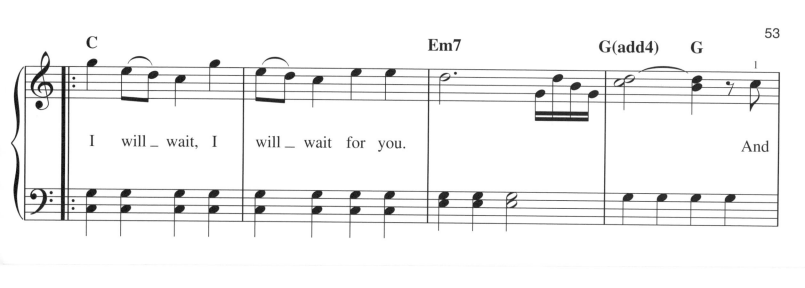

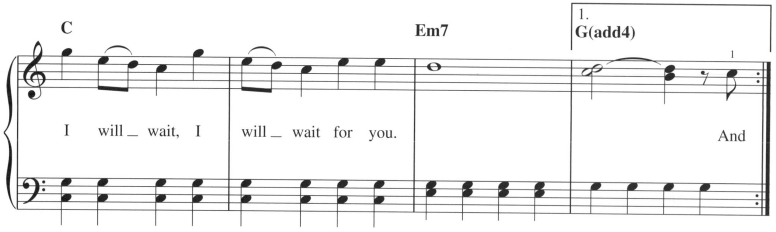

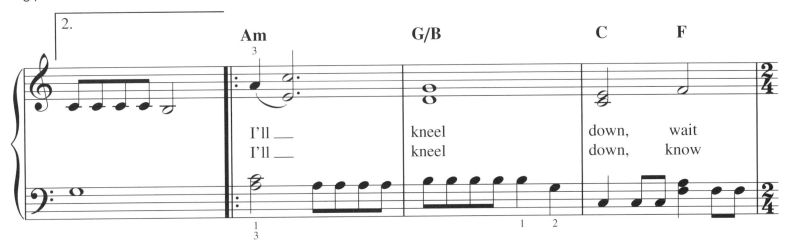

I'll — kneel down, wait
I'll — kneel down, know

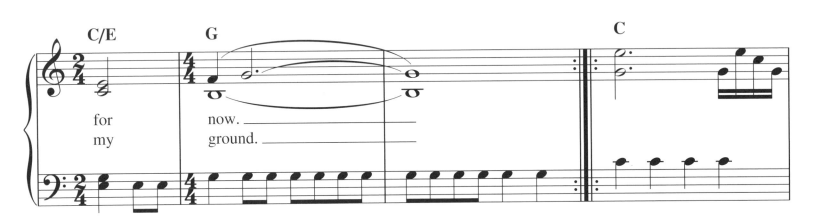

for now. —
my ground. —

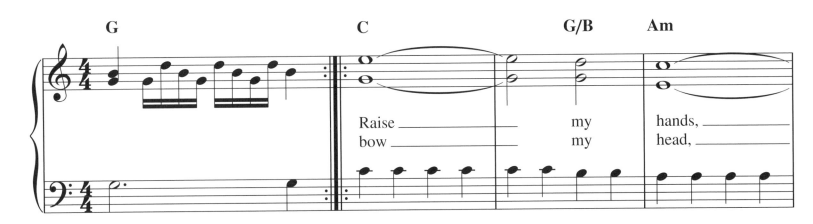

Raise — my hands, —
bow — my head, —

paint my spi - rit gold. ____ And
keep my heart ____ gold. ____

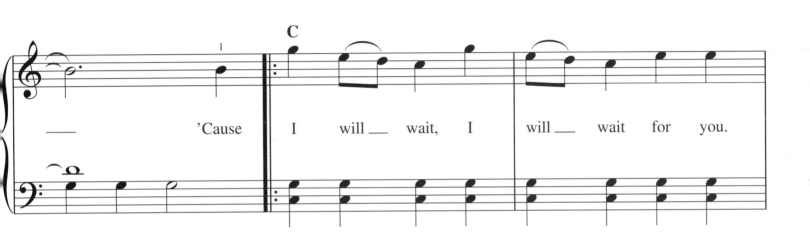

'Cause I will __ wait, I will __ wait for you.

And I will __ wait, I

will __ wait for you.

IT'S A BEAUTIFUL DAY

Words and Music by MICHAEL BUBLÉ,
ALAN CHANG and AMY FOSTER

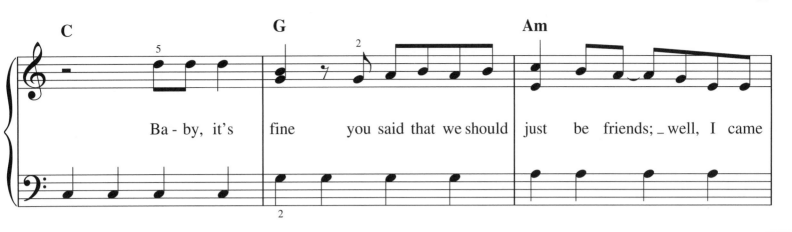

Ba - by, it's fine you said that we should just be friends; _ well, I came

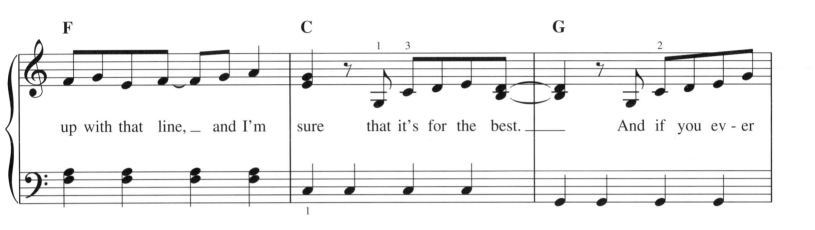

up with that line, _ and I'm sure that it's for the best. _____ And if you ev - er

change your mind, _ don't hold _____ your breath. _'Cause you may

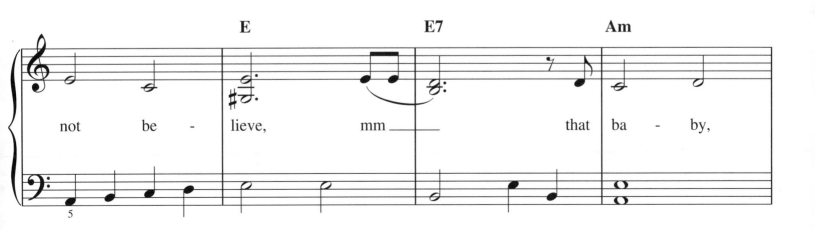

not be - lieve, mm _____ that ba - by,

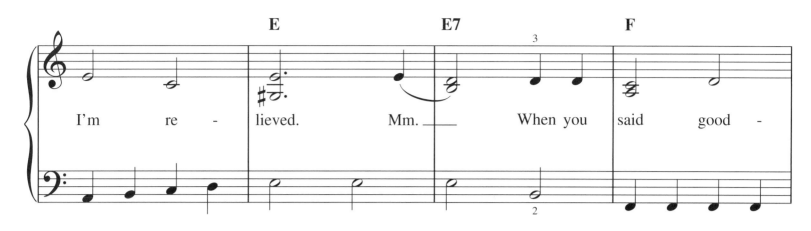

I'm re - lieved. Mm. When you said good -

bye, my whole world shined. Hey, hey, hey. It's a beau ti - ful day,

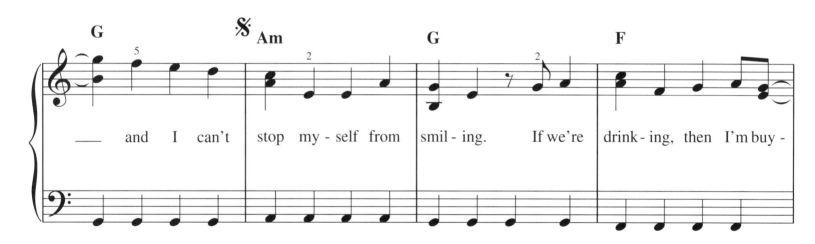

and I can't stop my - self from smil - ing. If we're drink - ing, then I'm buy -

- ing. And I know there's no de - ny - ing,

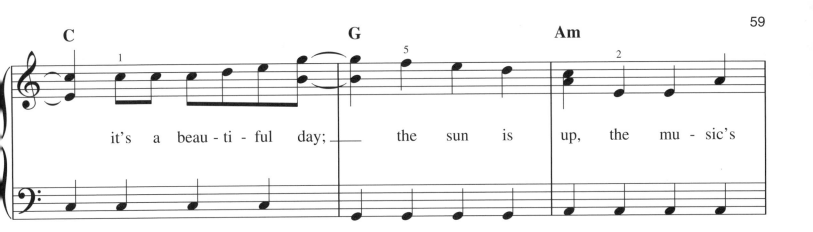

it's a beau - ti - ful day; ___ the sun is up, the mu - sic's

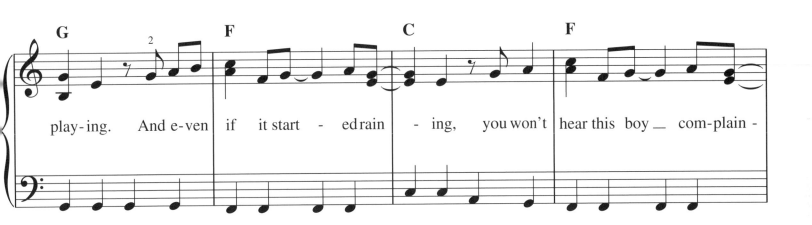

play-ing. And e-ven if it start - ed rain - ing, you won't hear this boy __ com-plain -

To Coda

- ing, 'cause I'm glad that you're _ the one ___ who got __ a - way. ___

It's a beau-ti - ful day. It's my turn to

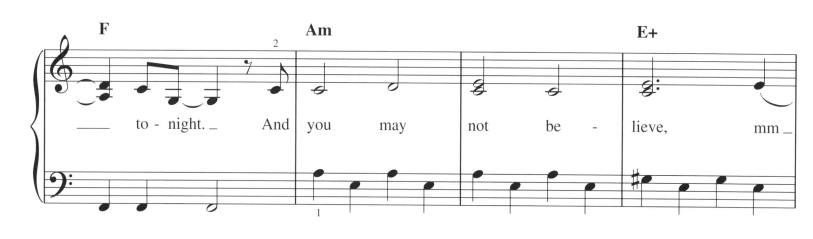

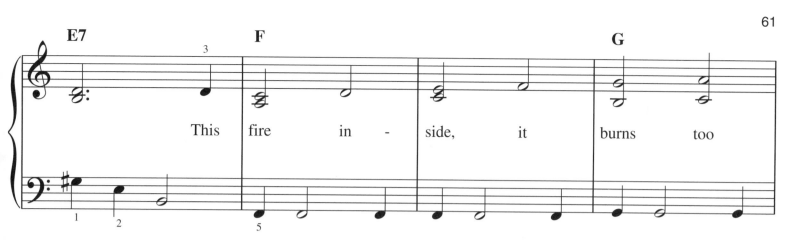

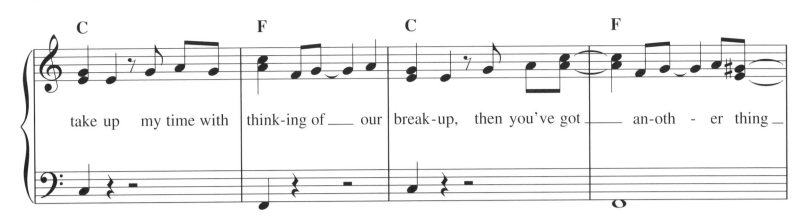

take up my time with think-ing of ___ our break-up, then you've got ___ an-oth - er thing ___

___ com-ing your way. ___ 'Cause it's a beau-ti - ful day, hey.

Beau-ti - ful day. ___ Oh

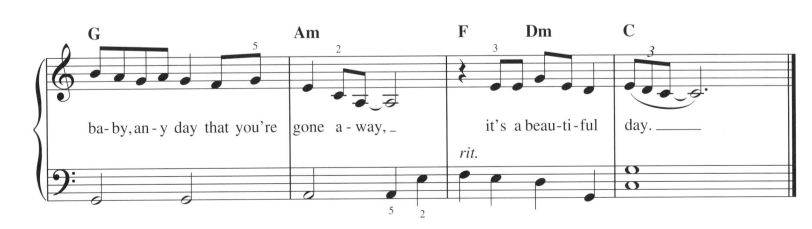

ba-by, an-y day that you're gone a - way, ___ it's a beau-ti-ful day. ___

JUST GIVE ME A REASON

Words and Music by ALECIA MOORE,
JEFF BHASKER and NATE RUESS

Right from the start you were a
Sor - ry. I don't un - der - stand where

thief, you stole my heart, and
all of this is com-ing from. I

I, your will - ing vic - tim.
thought that we were fine. ___

I
Your

let you see the parts of me that
head is run - ning wild a - gain. My

weren't all that pret - ty, ___ and with
dear, we still have ev - 'ry-thing, and

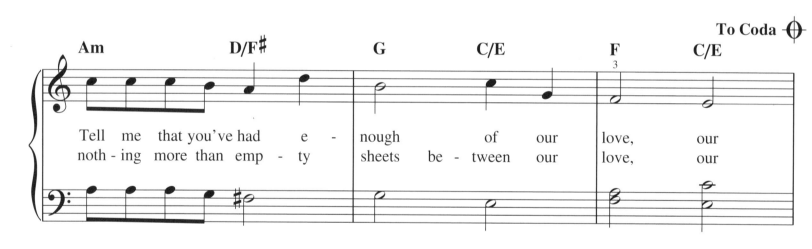

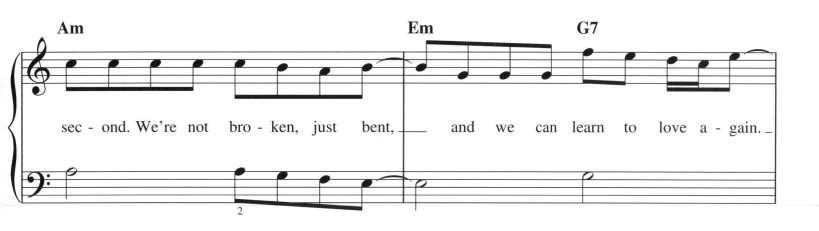

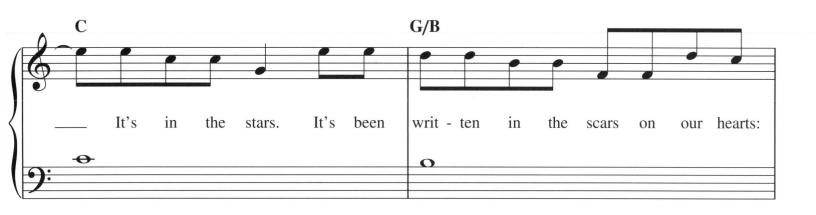

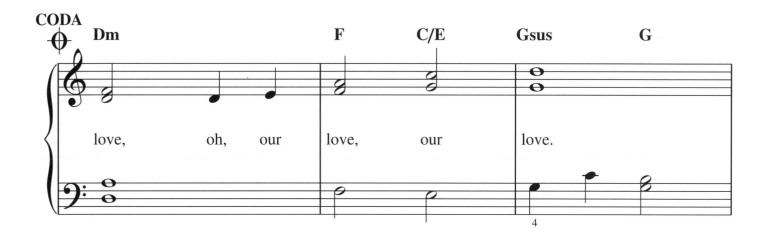

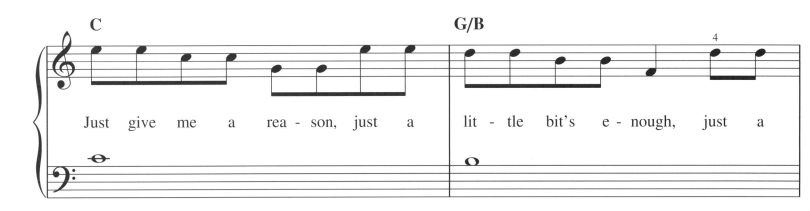

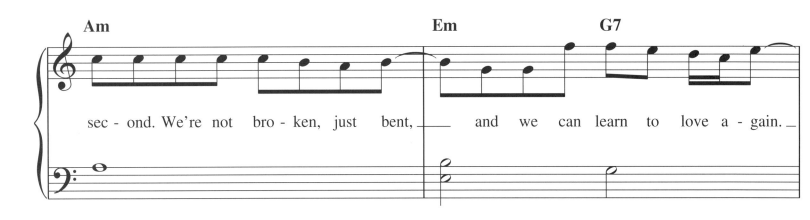

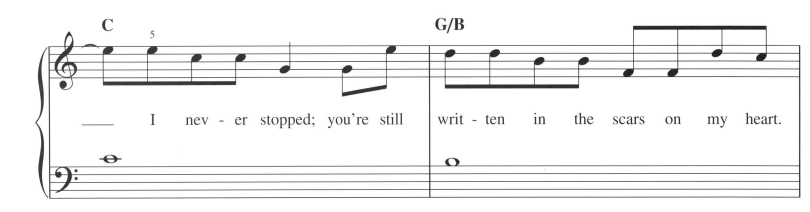

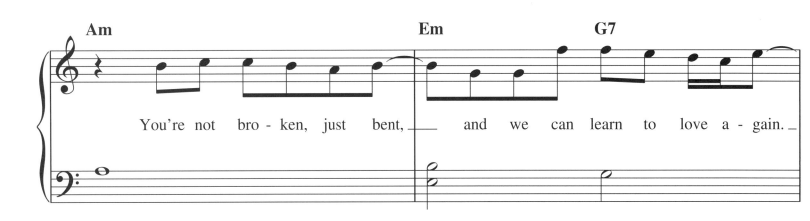

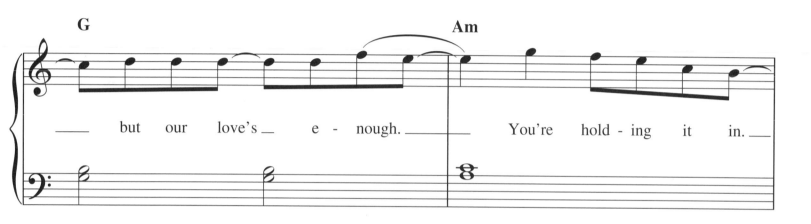

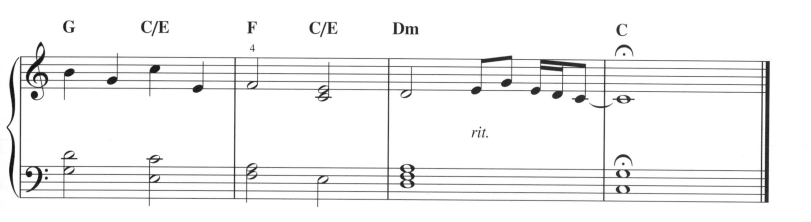

MIRRORS

Words and Music by JUSTIN TIMBERLAKE,
JAMES FAUNTLEROY, JEROME HARMON,
TIM MOSLEY, CHRIS GODBEY
and GARLAND MOSLEY

Aren't you some-

- thing to ad-mi - re? 'Cause your shine ___ is some-thing like a mir-
- thing, an or-i - gi-nal, 'cause it does - n't seem mere-ly as-sem-

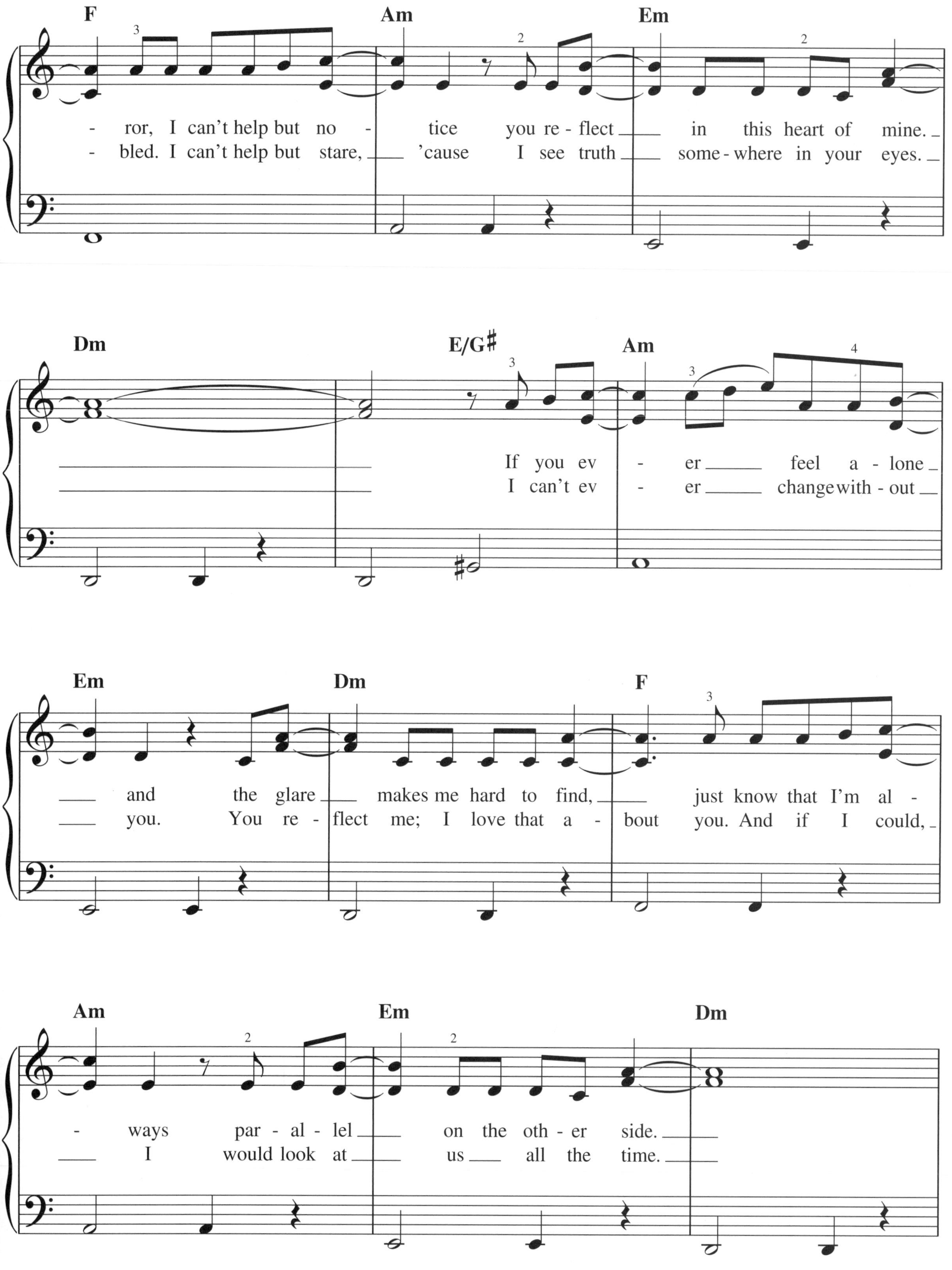
F
Am
Em
3
2
2
- ror, I can't help but no - tice you re - flect in this heart of mine.
- bled. I can't help but stare, 'cause I see truth some - where in your eyes.
Dm
E/G♯
Am
3
3
4
If you ev - er feel a - lone
I can't ev - er change with - out
Em
Dm
F
3
and the glare makes me hard to find, just know that I'm al -
you. You re - flect me; I love that a - bout you. And if I could,
Am
Em
Dm
2
2
- ways par - al - lel on the oth - er side.
I would look at us all the time.

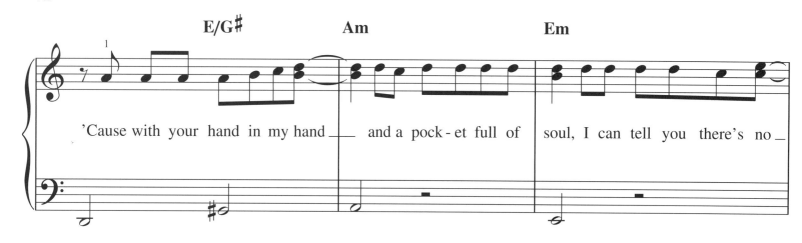

'Cause with your hand in my hand and a pock-et full of soul, I can tell you there's no

place we could-n't go. Just put your hand on the past, I'll be try'n' to pull you

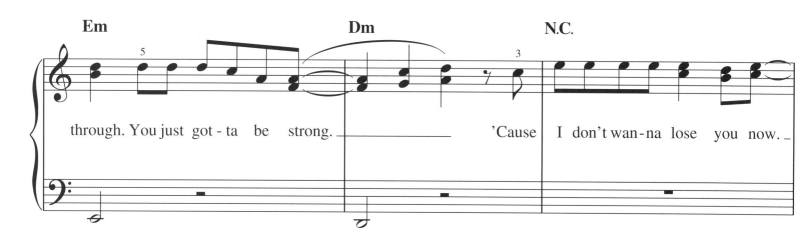

through. You just got-ta be strong. 'Cause I don't wan-na lose you now.

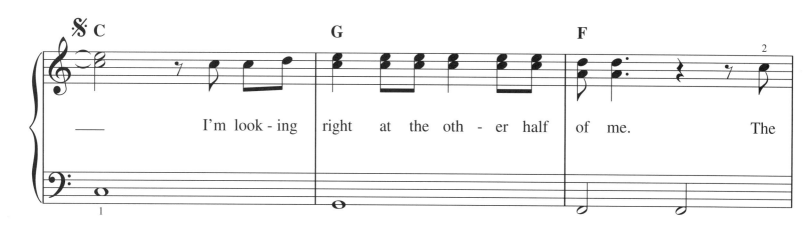

I'm look-ing right at the oth-er half of me. The

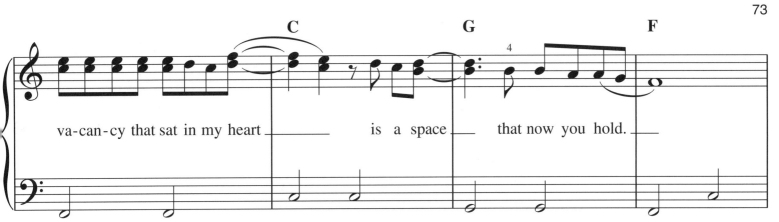

va-can-cy that sat in my heart _____ is a space ___ that now you hold. ____

Show me how to fight for now. ____ And I'll tell you, ba-by, it was eas - y com-ing back here

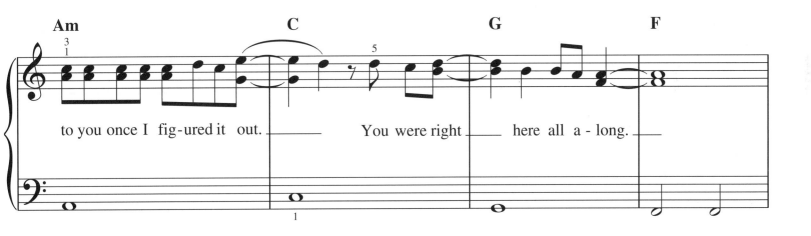

to you once I fig-ured it out. ____ You were right ___ here all a - long. ____

It's like you're my mir - ror, oh, _ my mir-ror star-ing back at me.

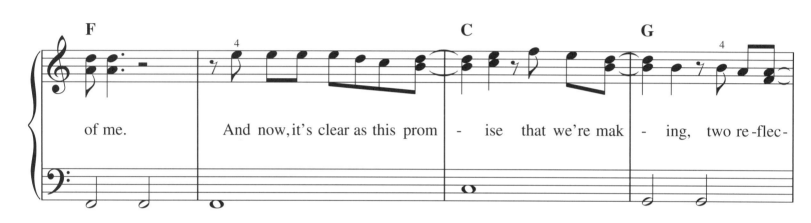

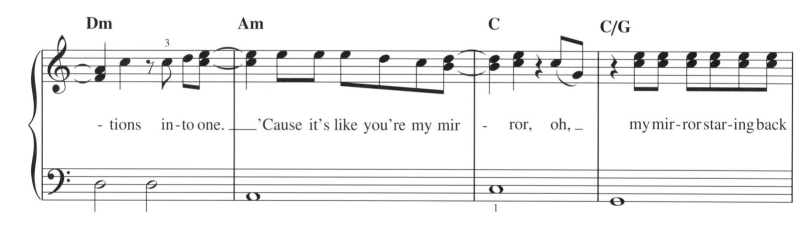

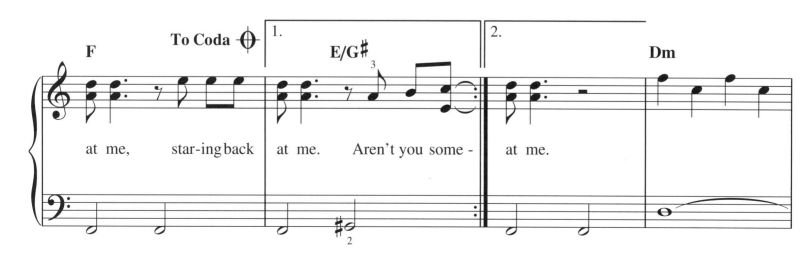

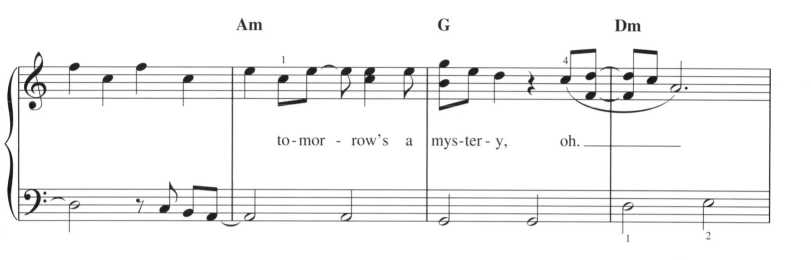

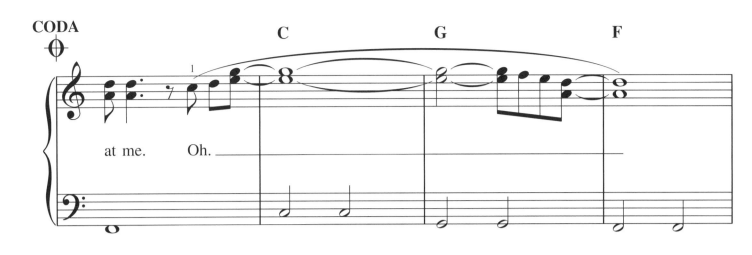

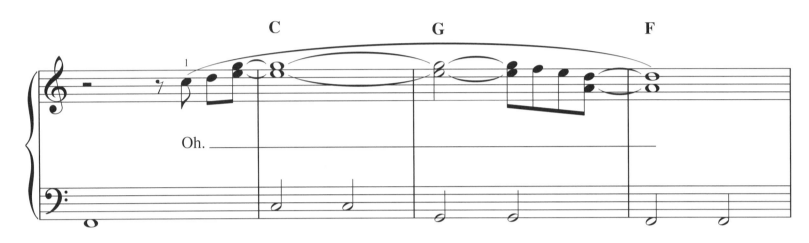

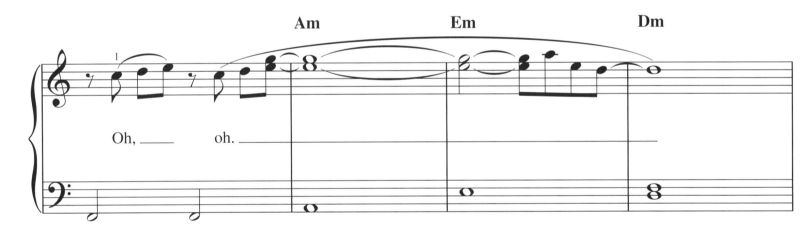

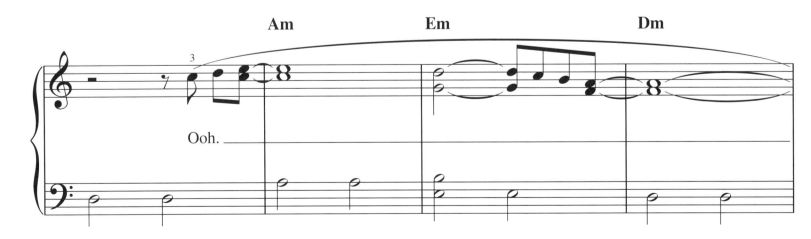

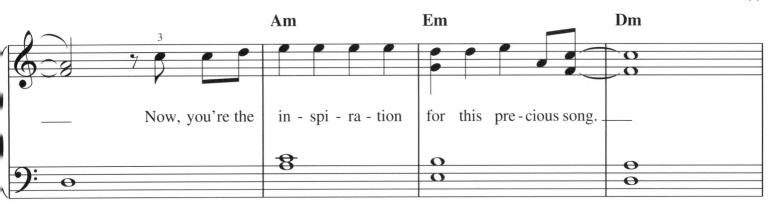

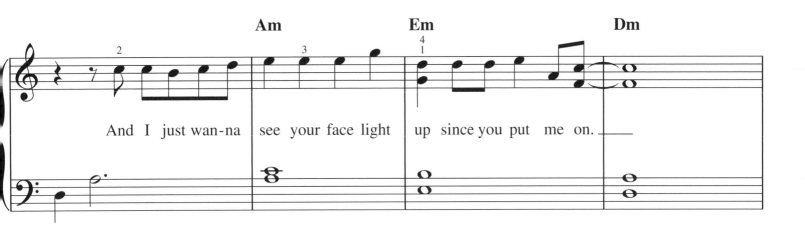

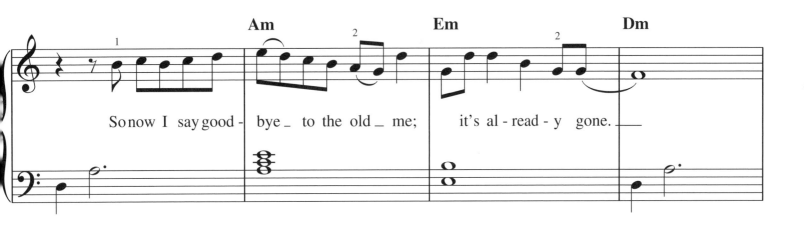

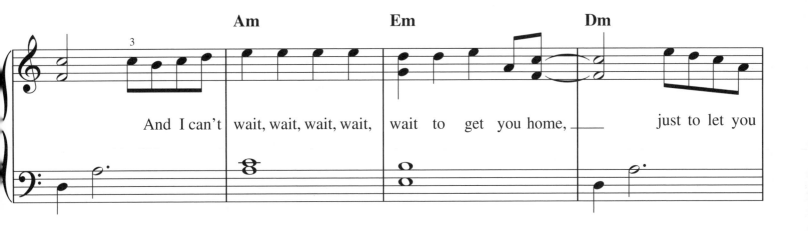

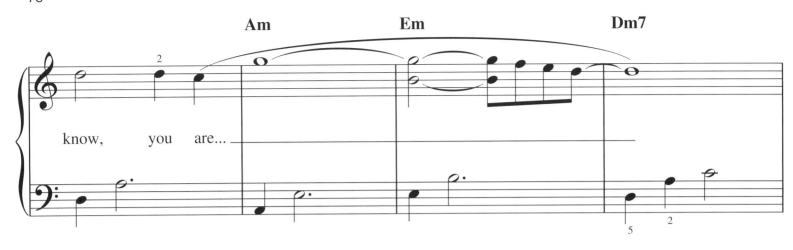

Am   Em   Dm7

know,   you   are...

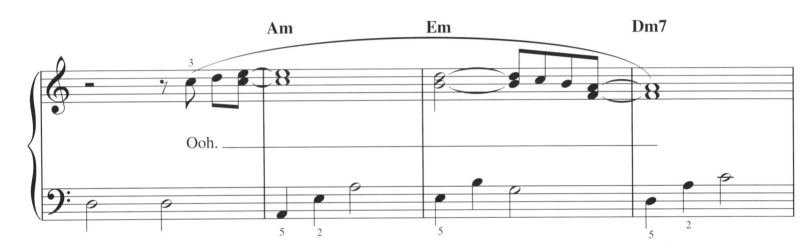

Am   Em   Dm7

Ooh.

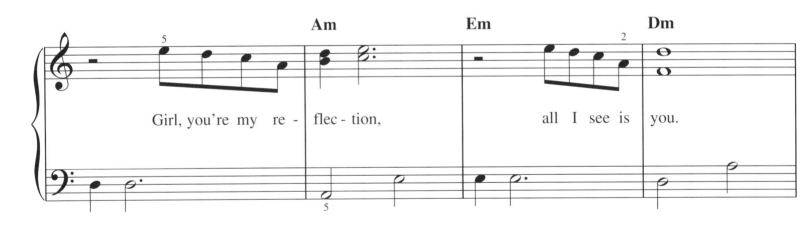

Am   Em   Dm

Girl, you're my re - flec - tion,   all I see is you.

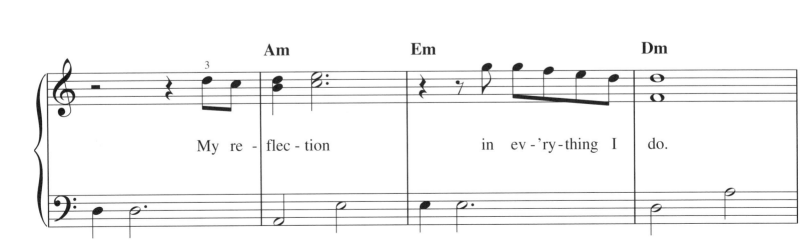

Am   Em   Dm

My re - flec - tion   in ev -'ry-thing I do.

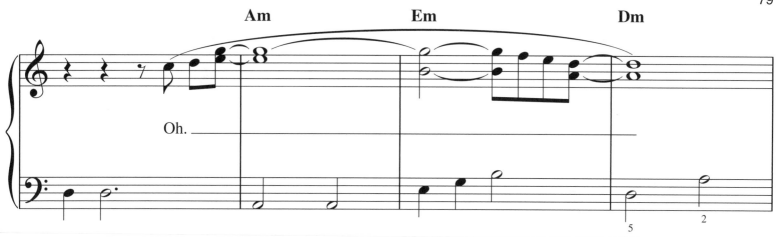

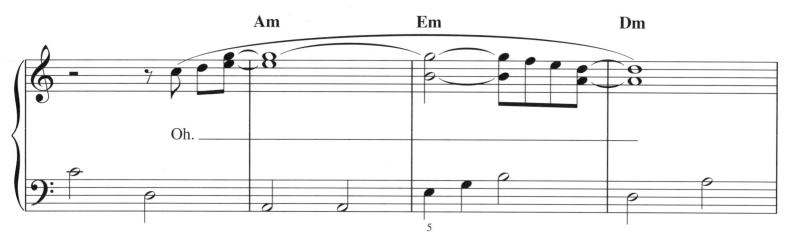

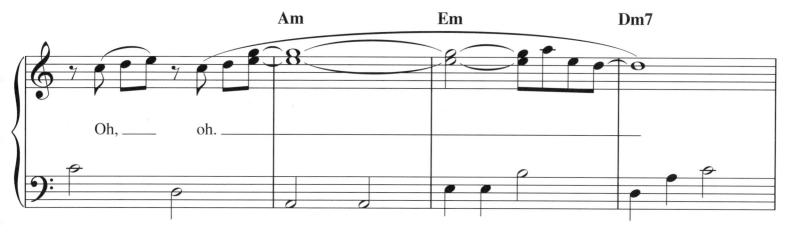

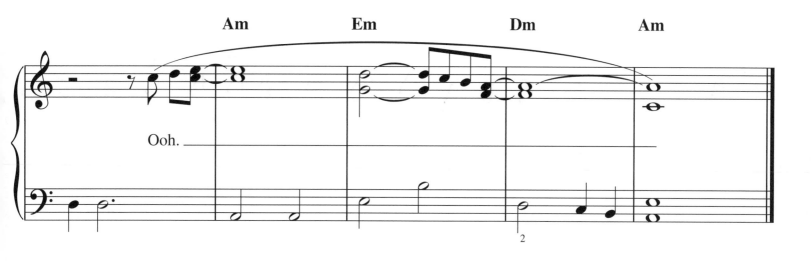

NEXT TO ME

Words and Music by EMELI SANDÉ,
HARRY CRAZE, HUGO CHEGWIN
and ANUP PAUL

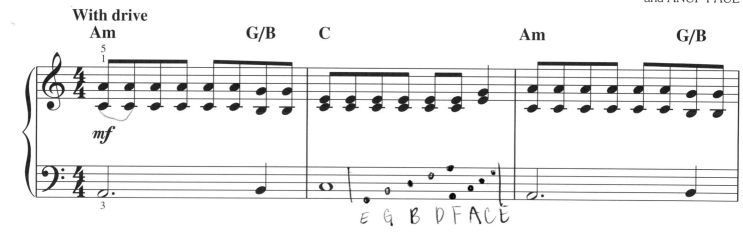

You won't find him drink-in' un-der ta-
mon-ey's spent and all my friends have van-

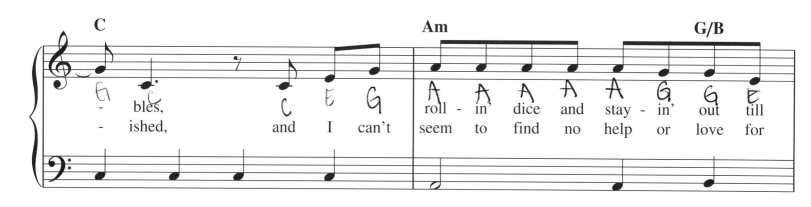

- bles, and I can't roll-in' dice and stay-in' out till
- ished, seem to find no help or love for

three. You won't ev-er find __ him bein' un-
free. I know there's no need __ for me to

faith - ful. You will find ___ him, you'll find ___ him next to me. ___
pan - ic, 'cause I'll find ___ him, I'll find ___ him next to me. ___

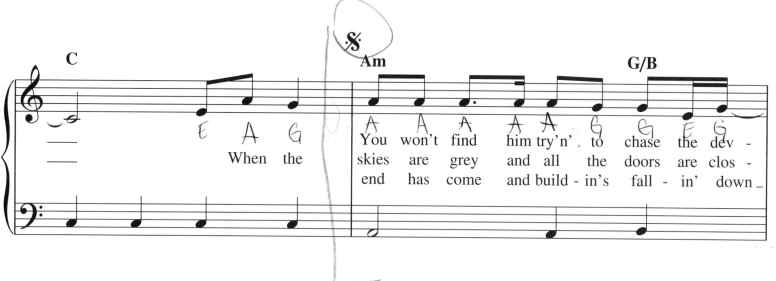

When the skies are grey and all the doors are clos -
end has come and build - in's fall - in' down ___

- il for mon - ey, fame, for pow - er out of
and the ris - ing pres - sure makes it hard to
fast, when we spoiled the land and dried up all the

greed. well, all I need's a hand to stop the tears from fall -
breathe, You won't ev - er find him where the rest ___
sea, when ev - 'ry - one has lost their heads a - round ___

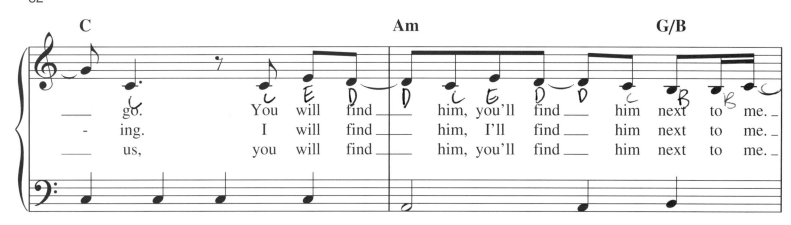

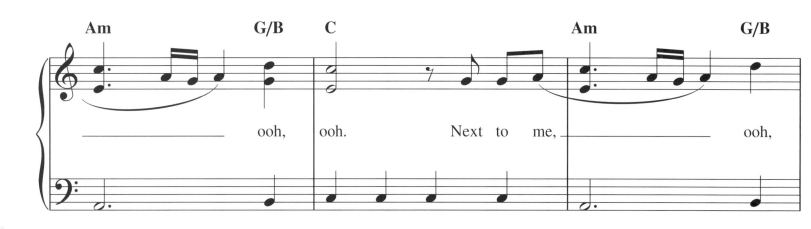

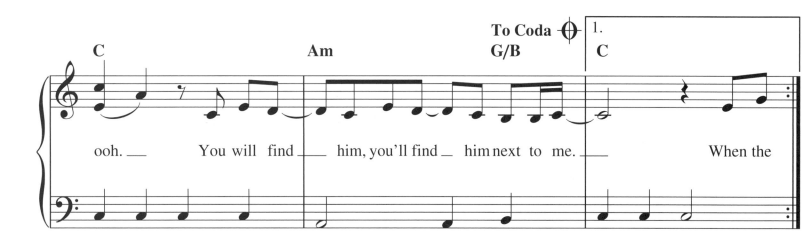

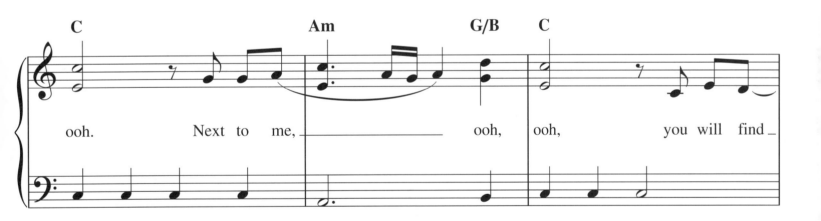

RADIOACTIVE

Words and Music by DANIEL REYNOLDS,
BENJAMIN McKEE, DANIEL SERMON,
ALEXANDER GRANT and JOSH MOSSER

rust.   I'm breath - ing in ____   the chem - i - cals. ____   Whoa, ____
pose.   We're paint - ed red ____   to fit right in. ____

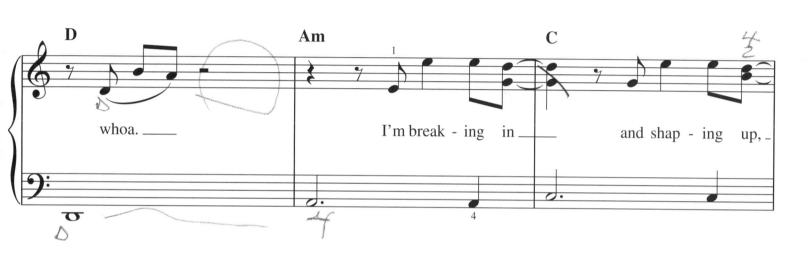

whoa. ____   I'm break - ing in ____   and shap - ing up, _

— then check - ing   out   on the pri - son bus.   This is   it, ____

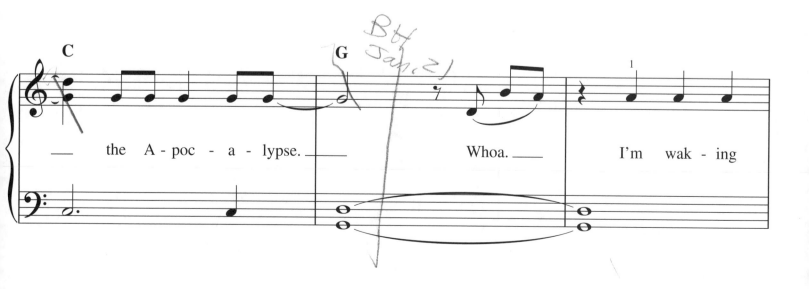

— the A - poc - a - lypse. ____   Whoa. ____   I'm wak - ing

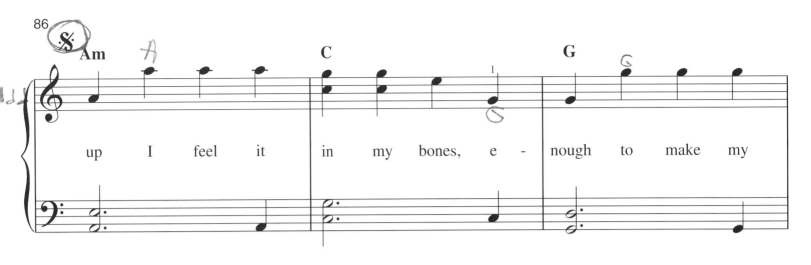

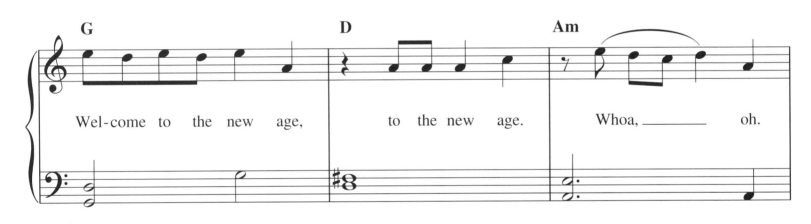

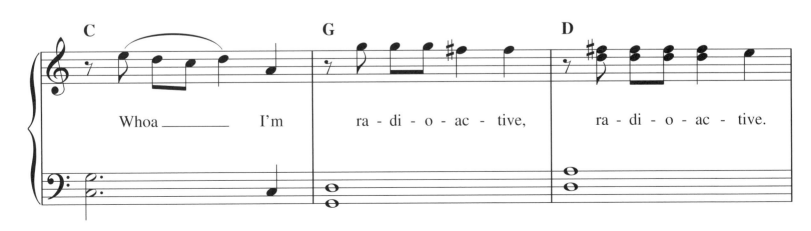

To Coda ⊕

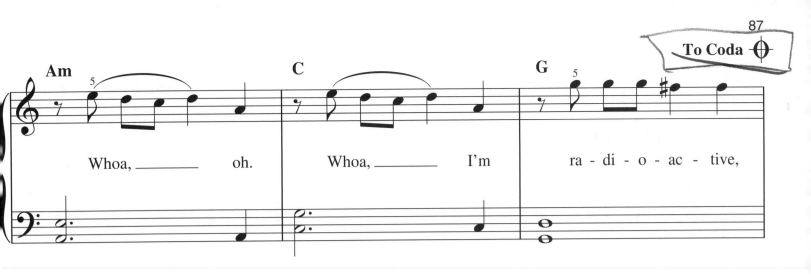

Whoa, _____ oh. Whoa, _____ I'm ra - di - o - ac - tive,

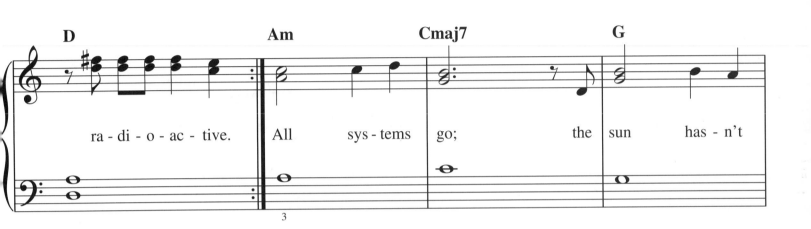

ra - di - o - ac - tive. All sys - tems go; the sun has - n't

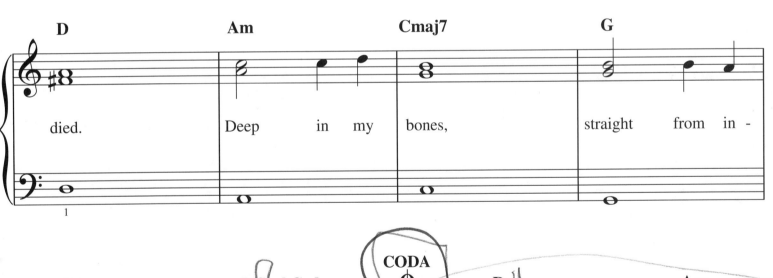

died. Deep in my bones, straight from in -

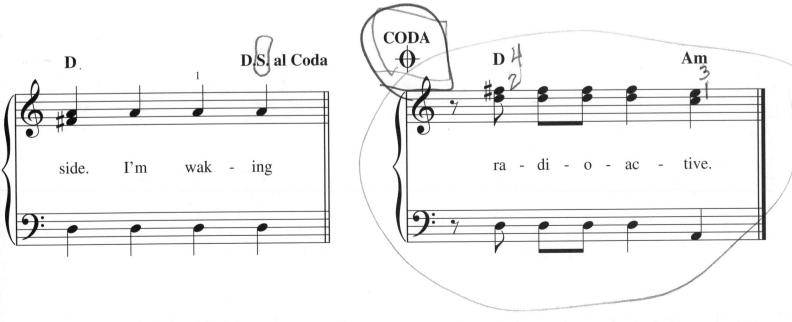

side. I'm wak - ing ra - di - o - ac - tive.

STAY

Words and Music by MIKKY EKKO
and JUSTIN PARKER

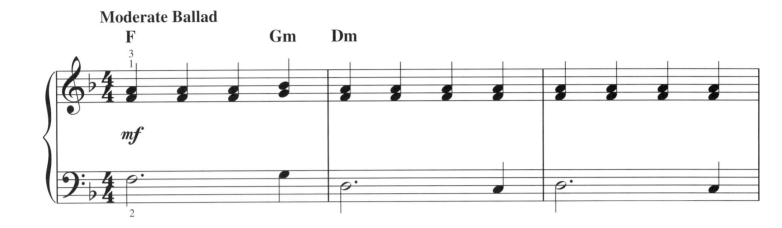

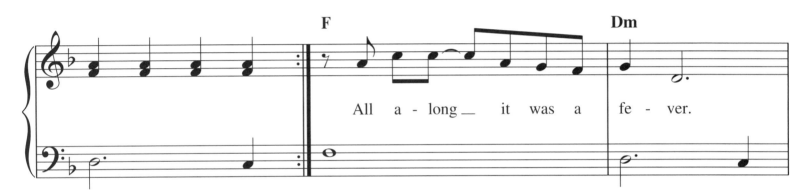

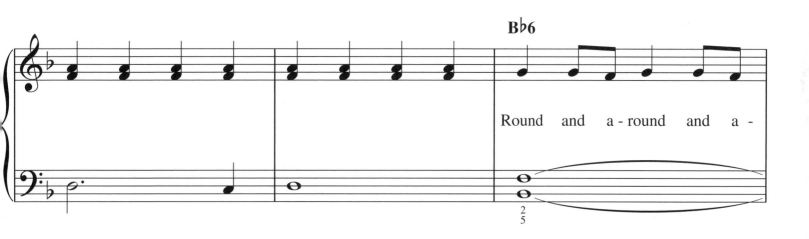

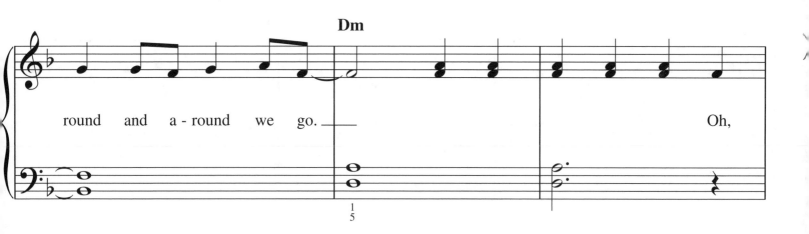

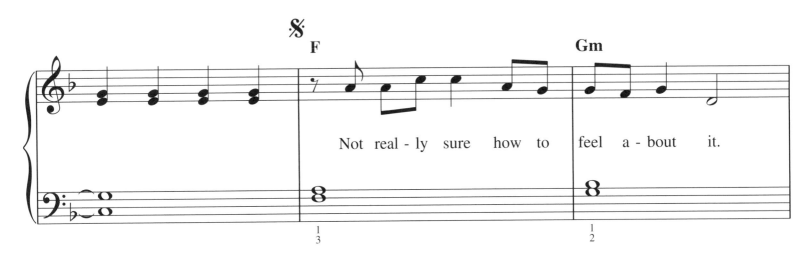

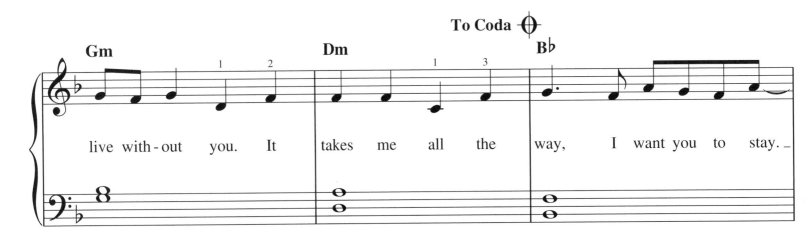

Fun - ny, you're the bro - ken one but

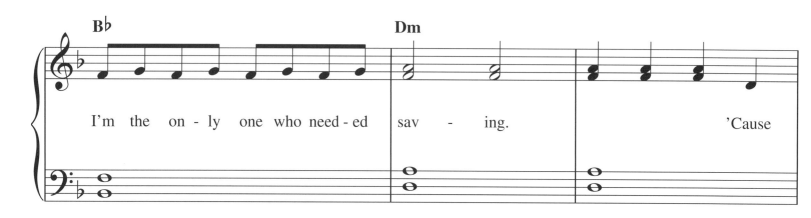

I'm the on - ly one who need - ed sav - ing. 'Cause

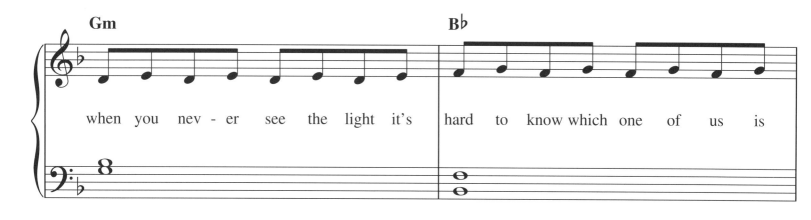

when you nev - er see the light it's hard to know which one of us is

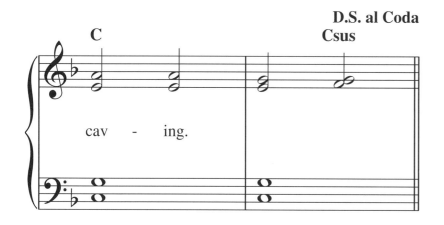

cav - ing.

way. I want you to stay, __

TRY

Words and Music by
BUSBEE and BEN WEST

Where there is de-

sire, there is gon - na be a flame. Where there is a

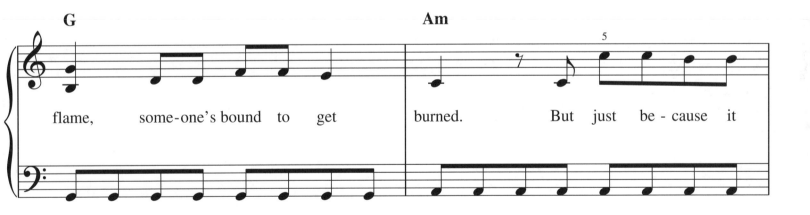

flame, some-one's bound to get burned. But just be - cause it

burns does - n't mean you're gon - na die; you got - ta get up

and try, try, try, got-ta get up and try, try,

try, gotta get up and try, try, try.

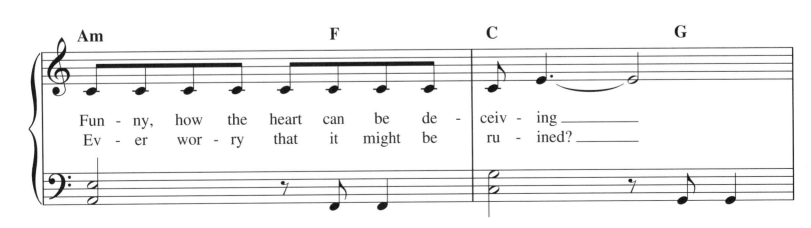

Fun - ny, how the heart can be de - ceiv - ing
Ev - er wor - ry that it might be ru - ined?

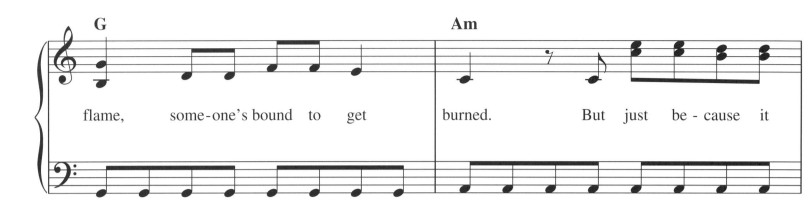

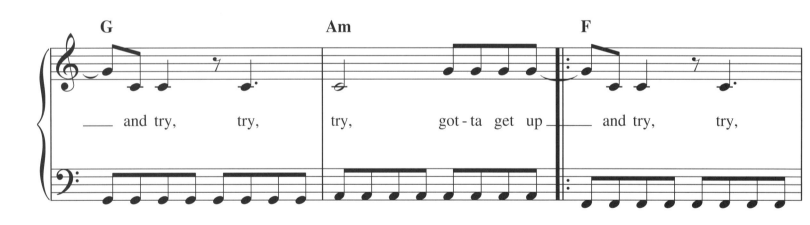

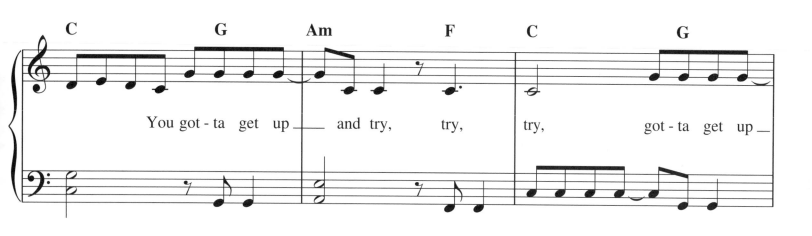

You gotta get up and try, try, try, gotta get up

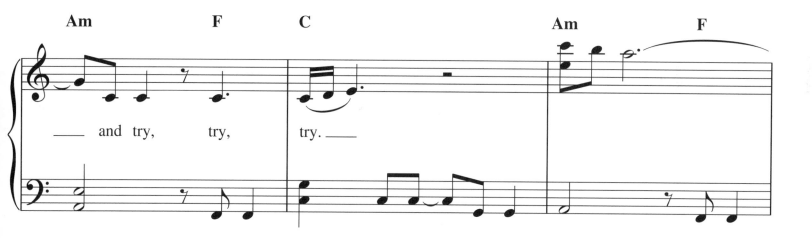

and try, try, try.

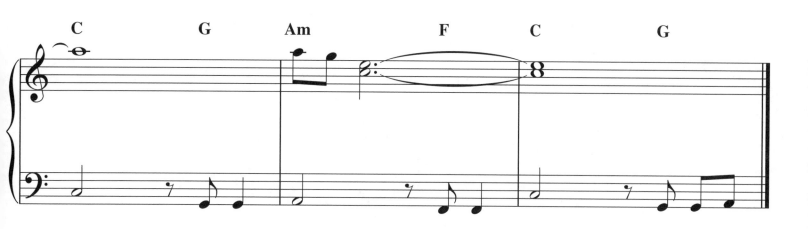

WE CAN'T STOP

Words and Music by MILEY CYRUS,
MICHAEL WILLIAMS, PIERRE SLAUGHTER,
TIMOTHY THOMAS, THERON THOMAS,
DOUGLAS DAVIS and RICKY WALTERS

Moderately slow Groove

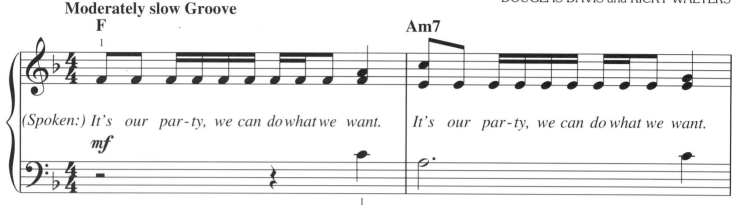

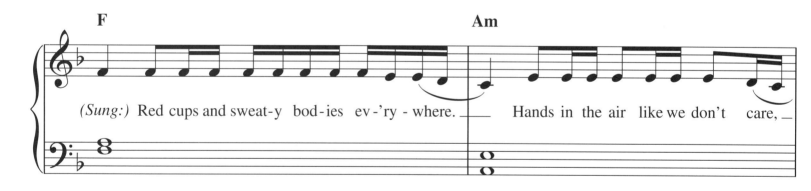

If you're not read-y to go home, ___ can I get a hell no? ___

___ 'Cause we gon-na go all night 'til we see the sun-light al-right. So,

la, da, di, da, di, we like to par-ty. Danc-in' with Mi-ley, do-in' what-ev-er we

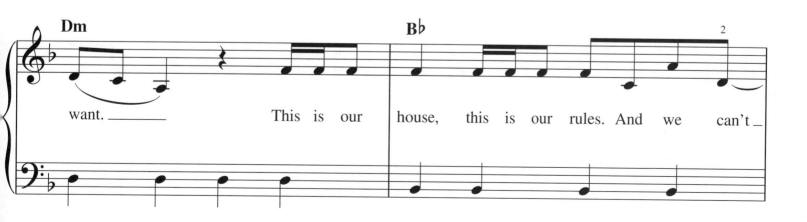

want. _____ This is our house, this is our rules. And we can't ___

stop. And we won't ____ stop. Can't you see it's

we who own the night. Can't you see it's me who 'bout the light. And we can't ____

____ stop. And we won't ____ stop. We run

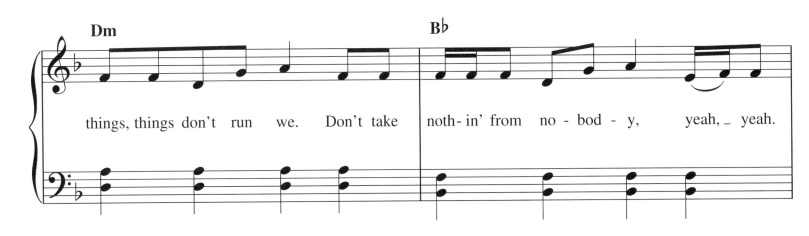

things, things don't run we. Don't take noth-in' from no - bod - y, yeah, _ yeah.

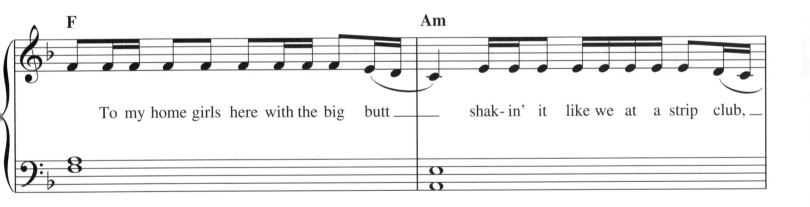

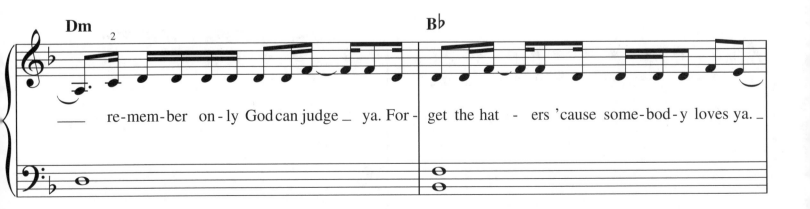

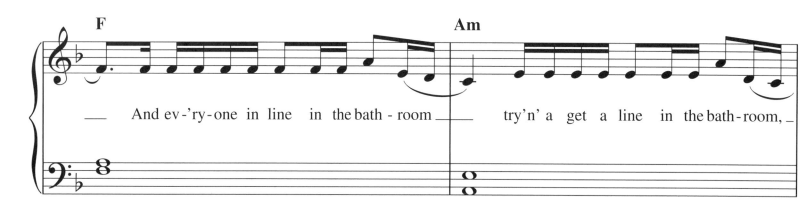

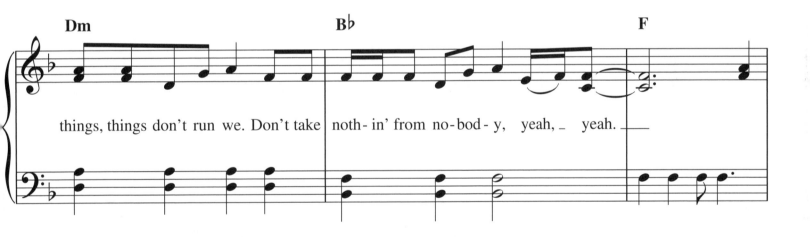

WHEN I WAS YOUR MAN

Words and Music by BRUNO MARS,
ARI LEVINE, PHILIP LAWRENCE
and ANDREW WYATT

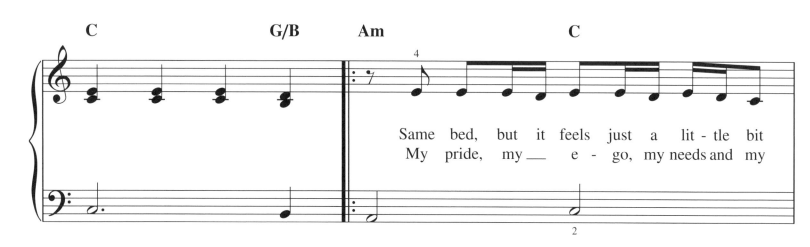

Same bed, but it feels just a lit-tle bit
My pride, my — e - go, my needs and my

big-ger   now. _____
self-ish   ways _____

Our   song   on the ra-di-o, but it don't
caused a good strong — wom-an like you to walk

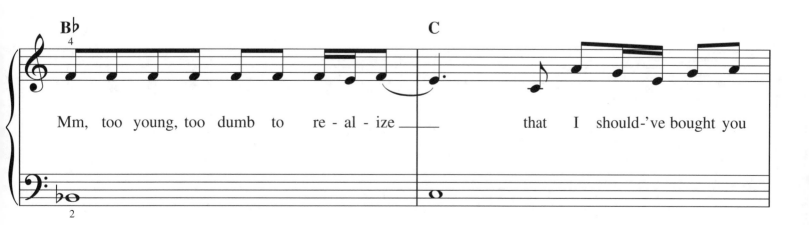

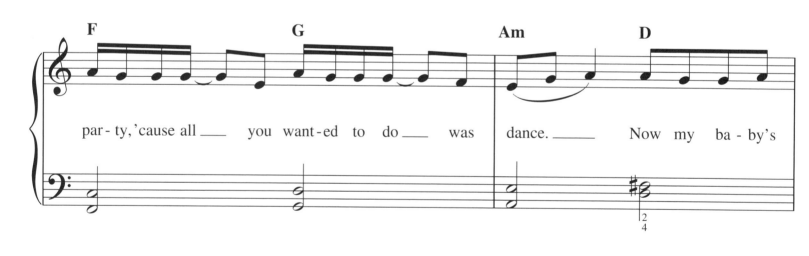

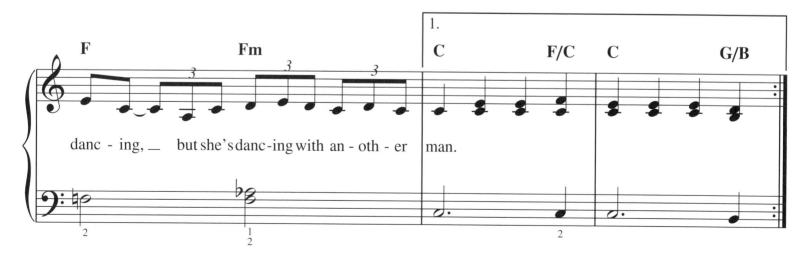

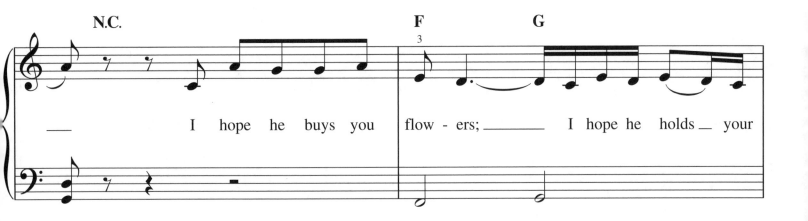

hand, give you all his hours _____ when he has the

chance; take you to ev-'ry par - ty, ___'cause I re-mem-ber how much _ you love

to dance; _ do all the things _ I _____ should-'ve done _ when I was your

man. Do all the things I _____ should-'ve done when I was your man.

rit.

It's Easy to Play Your Favorite Songs with Hal Leonard Easy Piano Books

Beatles Best for Easy Piano
Easy arrangements of 120 Beatles hits. A truly remarkable collection including: All My Loving • And I Love Her • Come Together • Eleanor Rigby • Get Back • Help! • Hey Jude • I Want to Hold Your Hand • Let It Be • Michelle • many, many more.
00364092....................... $24.99

The Best Broadway Songs Ever
The 2nd edition of this bestseller features 65+ Broadway faves: All I Ask of You • I Wanna Be a Producer • Just in Time • My Funny Valentine • On My Own • Seasons of Love • The Sound of Music • Tomorrow • Where or When • Younger Than Springtime • more!
00300178 .... $21.99

The Best Praise & Worship Songs Ever
The name says it all: over 70 of the best P&W songs today. Titles include: Awesome God • Blessed Be Your Name • Come, Now Is the Time to Worship • Days of Elijah • Here I Am to Worship • Open the Eyes of My Heart • Shout to the Lord • We Fall Down • and more.
00311312....................$19.99

The Best Songs Ever
Over 70 all-time favorite songs, including: All I Ask of You • Body and Soul • Call Me Irresponsible • Edelweiss • Fly Me to the Moon • The Girl from Ipanema • Here's That Rainy Day • Imagine • Let It Be • Moonlight in Vermont • People • Somewhere Out There • Tears in Heaven • Unforgettable • The Way We Were • and more.
00359223....................$19.95

Ten Top Hits for Easy Piano
Ten tunes from the top of the charts in 2006: Because of You • Black Horse and the Cherry Tree • Breaking Free • Jesus Take the Wheel • Listen to Your Heart • Over My Head (Cable Car) • The Riddle • Unwritten • Upside Down • You're Beautiful.
00310530................................ $10.95

Jumbo Easy Piano Songbook
200 classical favorites, folk songs and jazz standards. Includes: Amazing Grace • Beale Street Blues • Bridal Chorus • Buffalo Gals • Canon in D • Cielito Lindo • Danny Boy • The Entertainer • Für Elise • Greensleeves • Jamaica Farewell • Marianne • Molly Malone • Ode to Joy • Peg O' My Heart • Rockin' Robin • Yankee Doodle • dozens more!
00311014................................$19.99

Best Children's Songs Ever
A great collection of over 100 songs, including: Alphabet Song • The Bare Necessities • Beauty and the Beast • Eensy Weensy Spider • The Farmer in the Dell • Hakuna Matata • My Favorite Things • Puff the Magic Dragon • The Rainbow Connection • Take Me Out to the Ball Game • Twinkle, Twinkle Little Star • Winnie the Pooh • and more.
00310360................................ $19.95

150 of the Most Beautiful Songs Ever
Easy arrangements of 150 of the most popular songs of our time. Includes: Bewitched • Fly Me to the Moon • How Deep Is Your Love • My Funny Valentine • Some Enchanted Evening • Tears in Heaven • Till There Was You • Yesterday • You Are So Beautiful • and more. 550 pages of great music!
00311316................................$24.95

50 Easy Classical Themes
Easy arrangements of 50 classical tunes representing more than 30 composers, including: Bach, Beethoven, Chopin, Debussy, Dvorak, Handel, Haydn, Liszt, Mozart, Mussorgsky, Puccini, Rossini, Schubert, Strauss, Tchaikovsky, Vivaldi, and more.
00311215................................$12.95

Today's Country Hits
A collection of 13 contemporary country favorites, including: Bless the Broken Road • Jesus Take the Wheel • Summertime • Tonight I Wanna Cry • When I Get Where I'm Goin' • When the Stars Go Blue • and more.
00290188................................$12.95

VH1's 100 Greatest Songs of Rock and Roll
The results from the VH1 show that featured the 100 greatest rock and roll songs of all time are here in this awesome collection! Songs include: Born to Run • Good Vibrations • Hey Jude • Hotel California • Imagine • Light My Fire • Like a Rolling Stone • Respect • and more.
00311110................................$27.95

Disney's My First Song Book
16 favorite songs to sing and play. Every page is beautifully illustrated with full-color art from Disney features. Songs include: Beauty and the Beast • Bibbidi-Bobbidi-Boo • Circle of Life • Cruella De Vil • A Dream Is a Wish Your Heart Makes • Hakuna Matata • Under the Sea • Winnie the Pooh • You've Got a Friend in Me • and more.
00310322................................$16.99

Get complete song lists and more at **www.halleonard.com**
Prices, contents, and availability subject to change without notice

Disney characters and artwork © Disney Enterprises, Inc.

HAL•LEONARD®
CORPORATION

7777 W. BLUEMOUND RD. P.O. BOX 13819 MILWAUKEE, WI 53213

0512

THE GREATEST SONGS EVER WRITTEN

The Best Ever Collection
Arranged for Easy Piano with Lyrics.

The Best Acoustic Rock Songs Ever
64 songs: Against the Wind • American Pie • Barely Breathing • Change the World • Dust in the Wind • Free Fallin' • Have You Ever Seen the Rain? • I Will Remember You • Landslide • Maggie May • Night Moves • Superman (It's Not Easy) • Tears in Heaven • Yesterday • and more.
00311750.. $17.99

The Best Broadway Songs Ever
66 songs: All I Ask of You • Cabaret • Comedy Tonight • Don't Cry for Me Argentina • Getting to Know You • If I Were a Rich Man • Memory • Ol' Man River • People • Younger Than Springtime • and many more!
00300178.. $21.99

The Best Children's Songs Ever
102 songs: Alphabet Song • The Ballad of Davy Crockett • Bingo • A Dream Is a Wish Your Heart Makes • Eensy Weensy Spider • The Farmer in the Dell • Frere Jacques • Hello Mudduh, Hello Fadduh! • I'm Popeye the Sailor Man • Jesus Loves Me • The Muffin Man • On Top of Spaghetti • Puff the Magic Dragon • A Spoonful of Sugar • Twinkle, Twinkle Little Star • Winnie the Pooh • and more.
00310360.. $19.95

The Best Christmas Songs Ever
69 of the most-loved songs of the season: Auld Lang Syne • Blue Christmas • The Christmas Song (Chestnuts Roasting on an Open Fire) • Feliz Navidad • Grandma Got Run Over by a Reindeer • Happy Xmas (War Is Over) • I'll Be Home for Christmas • Jingle-Bell Rock • Let It Snow! Let It Snow! Let It Snow! • My Favorite Things • Old Toy Trains • Rudolph, The Red-Nosed Reindeer • Santa Claus is Comin' to Town • Toyland • You're All I Want for Christmas • and more.
00364130.. $19.95

The Best Contemporary Christian Songs Ever
50 songs: Awesome God • El Shaddai • Give Me Your Eyes • I Can Only Imagine • Live Out Loud • Only Grace • Place in This World • Testify to Love • Voice of Truth • and dozens more.
00312086 Easy Piano $19.99

The Best Country Songs Ever
78 songs, featuring: Always on My Mind • Could I Have This Dance • Crazy • Daddy Sang Bass • Forever and Ever, Amen • God Bless the U.S.A. • I Fall to Pieces • Jambalaya • King of the Road • Love Without End, Amen • Mammas, Don't Let Your Babies Grow Up to Be Cowboys • Paper Roses • Rocky Top • Sixteen Tons • Through the Years • Your Cheatin' Heart • and more.
00311540.. $17.95

The Best Easy Listening Songs Ever
75 songs: And I Love You So • Blue Velvet • Candle on the Water • Do You Know the Way to San Jose • Don't Cry Out Loud • Feelings • The Girl from Ipanema • Hey Jude • I Write the Songs • Just Once • Love Takes Time • Make the World Go Away • Nadia's Theme • One Voice • The Rainbow Connection • Sailing • Through the Years • Unchained Melody • Vincent (Starry Starry Night) • We've Only Just Begun • You Are So Beautiful • and more.
00311119.. $19.99

The Best Gospel Songs Ever
74 gospel songs, including: Amazing Grace • Blessed Assurance • Do Lord • Give Me That Old Time Religion • How Great Thou Art • I'll Fly Away • Just a Closer Walk with Thee • More Than Wonderful • The Old Rugged Cross • Precious Lord, Take My Hand (Take My Hand, Precious Lord) • Turn Your Radio On • The Unclouded Day • When the Roll Is Called up Yonder • Will the Circle Be Unbroken • and many more.
00310781.. $19.95

The Best Hymns Ever
116 hymns: Amazing Grace • Beneath the Cross of Jesus • Christ the Lord Is Risen Today • Down by the Riverside • For the Beauty of the Earth • Holy, Holy, Holy • It Is Well with My Soul • Joyful, Joyful We Adore Thee • Let Us Break Bread Together • A Mighty Fortress Is Our God • The Old Rugged Cross • Rock of Ages • Were You There? • and more.
00311120.. $17.95

The Best Jazz Standards Ever
71 jazzy tunes: Ain't Misbehavin' • Bye Bye Blackbird • Don't Get Around Much Anymore • Easy to Love • The Girl from Ipanema • It Don't Mean a Thing (If It Ain't Got That Swing) • The Lady Is a Tramp • My Funny Valentine • The Nearness of You • Old Devil Moon • Satin Doll • Stardust • Tangerine • and more.
00311091.. $17.95

The Best Movie Songs Ever
71 songs: Alfie • Beauty and the Beast • Born Free • Circle of Life • Endless Love • Theme from *Jaws* • Moon River • Somewhere Out There • Speak Softly, Love • Take My Breath Away • Unchained Melody • A Whole New World • and more.
00310141.. $19.95

The Best Praise & Worship Songs Ever
74 songs: Agnus Dei • Better Is One Day • Come, Now Is the Time to Worship • Days of Elijah • Firm Foundation • God of Wonders • Here I Am to Worship • I Can Only Imagine • Jesus, Lover of My Soul • Lamb of God • More Precious Than Silver • Open the Eyes of My Heart • Shine, Jesus, Shine • There Is a Redeemer • We Bow Down • You Are My King (Amazing Love) • and more.
00311312.. $19.99

The Best Rock Songs Ever
More than 60 favorites: All Shook Up • Born to Be Wild • California Dreamin' • Duke of Earl • Free Bird • Great Balls of Fire • Hey Jude • I Love Rock 'N Roll • Imagine • Let It Be • My Generation • Na Na Hey Hey Kiss Him Goodbye • Oh, Pretty Woman • Rock Around the Clock • Spinning Wheel • Takin' Care of Business • Under the Boardwalk • Wild Thing • and more.
00310444.. $17.95

The Best Songs Ever
71 must-own classics: All I Ask of You • Blue Skies • Call Me Irresponsible • Crazy • Edelweiss • Georgia on My Mind • Imagine • Love Me Tender • Moonlight in Vermont • My Funny Valentine • Piano Man • Satin Doll • Tears in Heaven • Unforgettable • The Way We Were • When I Fall in Love • and more.
00359223.. $19.95

HAL•LEONARD®
CORPORATION
7777 W. BLUEMOUND RD. P.O. BOX 13819 MILWAUKEE, WI 53213
www.halleonard.com

Prices, contents, and availability subject to change without notice. Not all products available outside the U.S.A.   0913